JOHN SINOR

Eleven Albatrosses
in My Bluebird Tree

Compiled and Edited
by Steve Barone

Illustrated by
Chuck Beebe

JOYCE PRESS INC.
SAN DIEGO, CALIFORNIA
1976

Most of the material in this book originally appeared in the San Diego Evening Tribune and various newspapers subscribing to Copley News Service. Special thanks is given for permission to reprint it.

INTRODUCTION

When Mr. Barone approached me with the idea of compiling a collection of my columns into a book, I wished him luck. Frankly, I couldn't see how he was going to make it coherent. Over the years of writing the thing, so many cats, dogs, birds, frogs, turtles, children, and other assorted strange creatures have touched my life, I was afraid such a book might leave the readers as confused as I am.

However, Mr. Barone persisted.

I have never pretended to understand editors.

As for the title, when Diane and I married she brought six children to the altar and I brought five. Now, children can be a joy, comfort, and good luck omens on the journey through life, and are welcomed the same as the albatross is welcomed by sailors on the open sea.

However, an albatross can also be an awful pain in the neck sometimes. Just ask the Ancient Mariner, or any of the rest of us ancient people.—THE AUTHOR

P.S.—The albatross is also known as the gooney bird.

Dedicated to my wife, Diane,
who went all the way to "Someday"
with me.

PART ONE

As everybody knows, books are usually divided into different parts. At least, that's the way the people at Joyce Press explained it to me.

So this is Part One of four parts. It covers the first quarter of the year–January, February and March.

That's about as complicated as things are going to get in here.

A Taste of Lunch and Life

It was such a simple afternoon.

The day was my day off, and I felt a need to spend part of it out of the house, away from the typewriter and the telephone, the doorbell and the doldrums. Spring fever gets me in its clutches earlier each year.

My oldest son was still on vacation from the university, so we planned the night before to spend the afternoon together.

I can't remember the last time we did that. It is exceptionally hard, it seems, to find the time to spend most of an entire day with just one of my children. But, I think it is also exceptionally rewarding, for both parties.

"Just come on over when you get up," I said, "and we'll bum around on the beach or something. I've got a few errands to do in the morning, then I'll be free."

Actually, to take the entire afternoon off meant skipping some chores that my wife would probably end up having to do later on.

But I did it, and I'm glad.

We drove away from the house about 11 a.m. in his car.

"Which way, dad?" he asked. I said: "I don't know. Why don't we head over by Crystal Pier."

At the beach, we parked, locked up the car, and walked down on the sand. The sun was out, but the wind off the sea was bitter cold. A girl in blue jeans was standing under the pier, playing a guitar which I doubt she could hear over the crash of the surf.

We walked silently at first. Then we began talking. We talked about nothing in particular, and about everything. A little bit of car talk, school talk, money talk. He asked if I still planned to look for a little beach house after all but a couple of the kids were gone. I said it was still just dream talk.

I said, "Hey, do you shoot pool?" He said: "Not too great. How about you?" I said: "So so." He said: "I'll bet."

We went into a nearby billiard parlor and I played the first four games of pool I'd ever played with him. Beat him just barely. I had two beers and he had a cola, and, on the way out of the place, we played a coin machine where you fire missiles at moving targets. He beat me.

He said: "Dad, I made some great beans last night. Onions, hamburger, mushrooms, all that stuff. You want to go over to my place and have some later on?"

I said: "Well, you know I have a pretty fragile stomach. Besides, I thought we might go to this place I know for some sea food." He said: "Out of sight.'

We had our lunch at an outdoor table at the edge of Quivira Basin, with a mass of anchored fishing and pleasure boats for our view.

Again we talked about this and that. About what he has done in the past, how he has tasted life. And about what he would like to do.

He wants to finish school. He wants to learn to fly. He would like to go to sea. It would be great to just roam around the country for a summer. He would like to act some more. He would like to write.

"There just isn't time," he said. "I want to do so many things. Sometimes I wish I could be 19-years-old for the next 20 years."

I thought to myself—a portrait of a young man in love with life.

We drove out Pt. Loma to the Cabrillo Monument. Climbed the lighthouse. Looked for gray whales. Studied the model of Cabrillo's ship and tried to figure out how big it really was. We decided on 45 to 50 feet, and he paced the distance off in the Visitor's Center to get a better idea. (As he paced away from me, I thought: My, that boy is bow-legged.)

We walked outside, took a few more deep breaths of the chilled sea air, and drove home.

As he dropped me off, he said: "Thanks, dad." I said, "Thank you."

Nothing much really happened all afternoon. And I wouldn't have missed it for the world.

You Can Fool Some of the People
—for a few years

A gray weekend. I borrowed a saw from a neighbor and cut up the Christmas tree. Started a crackling fire and sent the last traces of the holiday season up in smoke.

An older son gave me a carton of crystals to sprinkle on the fire. It turns the flames to colors.

This amazes the youngest child. I say: "Watch this. Presto! Ka-Zam!" The fire turns blue, red and green."

She thinks I am a magician.

Sometimes, when we pick up her mother at work, I do a few tricks for her while waiting in the car.

I make coins disappear right before her eyes. Then I shake them out of her ears.

She giggles like crazy. "How do you do that?" she asks.

"Pure magic," I say.

Then I tell her to cup her hands under her chin. I shake her nose and pennies jiggle down into her palms.

"What a funny place to keep money," I say. "Don't you have a purse?"

This drives her into hysterics.

When I was in short pants, I adored magicians. I think every boy wants to be a magician at some time during his life. I wanted to be Harry Houdini.

I bought a book about him at the magic store.

That Houdini could get out of anything. The book never told how he did it. I supposed it just took lots of practice.

I had a pal named Lester who lived next door tie my wrists behind my back with ropes. "Tie 'em up tight Lester," I said.

Lester tied 'em up too tight.

A half hour later, I was still struggling. And my hands were numb from lack of circulation.

I told Lester to untie me. I figured I'd better start on card tricks.

Whatever happened to magic stores, anyway?

Some time during those years, I bought a device for throwing your voice. I sent away for it with a coupon from the back of a comic book.

"Be A Ventriloquist!" the ad said. "Amaze Your Friends!"

There was a picture of a grinning kid, a small box with the word "Help!" coming from it, and an amazed friend standing nearby.

The device cost 25-cents, so I figured it had to work.

When I got the thing in the mail, I put it in my mouth and went out to amaze my friends.

I said: "Helf! Helf!" (You had to put the thing under your tongue, and it was hard to speak clearly.)

Grandma said: "What's the matter with you, boy? I can't understand a word you're saying."

Now I am older and wiser and a lot more magical. I have learned that the real trick to magic is careful selection of your audience.

I do not try to fool grandmothers. I do not try to amaze my friend next door.

I concentrate on 5-year-olds. They usually work just fine.

I said: "Watch now. I'll make a quarter pop right out of your nose."

She said: "I saw it! I saw it in your hand!"

I said: "You know, you may be getting a little too old for magic."

A Little Poetry—A Little Cheese

Still winter and cold, but there's a burst of camellias in the front yard. A washed blue sky over our green hills.

Maybe it is Indian Spring.

I hung a couple of new calendars over the desk where I give blood each day. Wondered what the dates will bring.

(I still find it hard to believe a lot of what happened last year.)

This year three more children in this household will graduate from high school. The Board of Education will kick them off the top branch with instructions: "Now fly!"

They said: "What will you write about when we're *all* gone?"

I said: "Who said I will write when you're all gone? Maybe your mother and I will buy a flashy sports car and join the social rumble. Maybe I will just sit on some bank and fish. Maybe . . ."

They said: "What we need around here is a new little brother."

I said: "Maybe I will join the French Foreign Legion."

The wife said: "Yeah, and maybe I'll join with you."

They said: "I know. We could all bring *our* children over to the house, and you could write about them."

I told the wife: "Look through the yellow pages there. See if there's a listing for the foreign legion."

I said: "Maybe your mother and I will get ourselves a garret in Paris and write poetry, paint, eat cheese."

She said: "I think the foreign legion sounds better."

They said: "If we can't have a baby brother, could we have a puppy?"

I said: "Ask you mother."

January turned to spring. (I hestitate to put words like that on paper. It sometimes seeds a storm.) Anyway, to press with sunshine and birdsong out the window.

Here's the sunny story of Old Harry, a skidrogue of Northern California a few years back.

Harry had a record of more than 60 arrests for being drunk. Each new one brought him 90 days in the slammer.

One morning, Harry appeared before the municipal judge and surprised the courtroom by pleading "not guilty" to the "common drunk" charge.

The judge said: "Harry, what can you mean? You got out of jail yesterday morning after serving 90 days, and were back in jail by the afternoon, as drunk as a lord."

Harry said: "Your honor, how can you accuse me of being a common drunk? That's the first time I've been drunk in three months."

Case dismissed.

No Dragon Ladies Here

We are approaching Chinese New Year. Gung Hay Fat Choy!

This will be the Year of the Pig. A very fine year to be born. Pig people are chivalrous and gallant. Also brave and very honest.

If you were born in 1935 or 1947 you are a Pig person. (Don't marry a Snake person. They are nothing but bad news for you.)

Much Oriental tradition is tied up in the calendar. It tells them when to marry, whom to marry, whom to run from.

It's considered such bad luck to have a girl born in the Year of the Dragon that China's birth rate drops by the hundreds of thousands in those years.

For Dragon ladies tend to pop off their husbands at an alarming rate.

(If your wife was born in 1916, 1928, 1940, or 1952, don't say you weren't warned.)

I am a Horse person. We Horse people are popular, cheerful, skillful with money, and perceptive. It says so right in my files.

I said to the wife: "Did you realize I am all these things?"

She said: "Doesn't it say anything bad about Horse people?"

I said: "Oh, it says we may talk a little too much, but we are also wise, talented and confident. You lucky girl."

She said: "What am I?"

I said: "You, my dear, are a Snake person. You Snake people tend to overdo. You distrust other people's judgments, and you are inclined to be a bit fickle. We Horse people really should marry Tigers, Dogs or Sheep, but you Snakes are listed as 'next best.' "

"How nice," she hissed.

I am a nut on Chinese and Cantonese food. I like almost everything on the menu.

(One time I even got enough courage to order bird's nest soup. But I was relieved to find you had to place the order two days in advance.)

On Chinese New Year's Day I will go out and order Mm Heung Ngau Yuk (Five fragrances beef), almond and pea chow yuk, and maybe a little fire duck.

(I may take a Snake to dinner with me, if she watches her step.)

On Chinese New Year's Day you should pay all your bills, dress in clean clothes, get a haircut. (I said: "Did you boys hear that?")

Don't go to the doctor on New Year's Day. Don't even talk about feeling bad. Or you will. For it is very bad luck.

Buy some flowers. Give children money. (They said: "We heard *that*!")

Don't break dishes. Don't clean the house. Don't sew. Be nice.

I looked up all the years of the children. We have almost all the animals. Sheep, Monkey, Horse, Chicken.

Our only Dragon is a boy. Thank goodness!

I've Got a Secret

A few days of pure gold. Flags snapping in the warm breeze. Blue skies and sun-splashed beaches and parks.

I was walking hand-in-hand down the sunny sidewalk the other day with a certain cupcake, when she asked me: "Can you keep a secret?"

"Me? Keep a secret?" I said: "Are you kidding? I have been cleared by the FBI to keep secrets. I can keep *top secrets*!"

This is a true story. (A true war story by the silver-haired old veteran.)

During the Korean War, I was assigned to a brand new air force base. It was so new, it hadn't even been built yet. I was the 18th person assigned to it.

"We'll have to get you a top secret clearance," said my officer-in-charge. "The first hundred people on a base are considered 'key personnel' and have to have the clearance."

I was only a 20-year-old sergeant in charge of putting out the base newspaper, but I thought to myself: "Oh boy, the Air Force is going to tell me some secrets."

I figured maybe they were going to let me look over the plans for building an atom bomb or something.

It took the FBI something like six months to approve the clearance. I mean, a top secret clearance is no easy thing to get. Not many generals have one.

They went around asking my high school buddies and former bosses all kinds of questions about me.

Had anyone ever seen me trying to overthrow the government?

Was I suspicious in any way?

Did I keep secrets well?

Finally, after all those months, my service record was duly stamped and recorded: "Cleared for Top Secret."

I figured it was only a matter of time before I was called in to conference somewhere to sit down and help plan the war.

Up to that time, I had only seen "restricted" material, which is kind of low-grade secret stuff that anybody but civilians is allowed to read.

Things like the daily mess hall menu, and what was playing at the base movie.

Well, during my three years in the Air Force, I was never told one single secret. Not one. (It seemed a shame. Here I was, somebody people could talk to. But nobody talked.)

However, my service record followed me from base to base. And the top secret clearance went with it.

It drove my superiors at other bases mad.

There was no explanation on the record as to *why* I had the clearance. And they didn't have a top secret clearance. How come one of their men did?

One colonel accused me of being a CIA man posing as an enlisted man.

I gave him a sort of mysterious smile, and was assigned the best room in the noncommissioned officers' barracks.

So, all these years later, I whispered to the cupcake: "Your secret will be in the best of hands. What is it?"

She said: "Cynthia is my best friend."

I said: "I see. Well, they couldn't drag it out of me with a rubber hose. My lips are sealed."

Balmy days around here. Spring seems right around the corner. And if I knew which corner, I would go for a walk.

"Isn't it nice to start getting longer days?" said the wife. "Look how much light we have left at five-thirty."

I said: "Look at the clock again. It's only four-thirty."

Still, the clock is ticking. The calendar is flipping. And I can already smell beach days, rosebuds, and blue barbecue smoke.

We expect to have more beach time this year. Congress has shuffled around a lot of holidays so they fall on Monday this year. George Washington got a new birthday. The date Columbus discovered America has been altered.

"We get out of school February 2nd," said the children. "It's the semester break."

There you have something. The school kids have out-negotiated the labor unions. Now they get Groundhog Day off.

Soft Glow of the Panic Light

A student's distress call sounded through the household: "Where's the typewriter? Melinda's coming over for her typewriter, and I can't find it *any*where! And she's coming right over! She's *got* to have it!"

The panic light glows warmly.

I started to say, "Where did you put it?" but that is about the most useless question I know.

I said: "Where all have you looked? Did you look under the bed? Did you look in the freezer?"

"What would a typewriter be doing in the freezer?"

I said: "Don't ask me. Last week I found a peanut butter sandwich in my sock drawer. Nothing would surprise me."

She said: "It was probably stolen. We probably had a burglar. What'll I say?"

Her mother found the typewriter behind the couch. (I don't know why we didn't look there first. Doesn't everybody keep typewriters behind the couch?)

She said: "I wonder who put it there?"

I said: "Probably the burglar. He probably planned to pick it up later."

We have our own personal burglar. Of course, we can't *prove* we have a burglar. But, prove it or not, he gets a lot of blame for missing items around here.

"I positively *know* I put the good silver in the bottom drawer of the hutch. And now it's gone. Somebody *had* to take it."

I said: "The Burglar?"

She said: "Well, the neighbors said there was a rumor a cat burglar was working in the neighborhood."

I said: "Good. Maybe he'll take some of the cats."

"Don't be silly," she said. "Something had to happen to the silver. Maybe we ought to call the police."

I said: "Wait a few days. It may show up in my sock drawer. Or in the freezer."

The phone rang. "Do we still have the club's big coffee maker?" I said. "Jonathan wants to come over and pick it up." She said: "Oh, Lord!"

The coffee maker *could* be down in the basement, I was told. (Of course, it could have been taken by the burglar.) "I haven't seen it since we moved," she said.

I found the coffee maker. It was in a box in the basement. It was in the same box with the good silver.

"I wonder how it got down there?" she said. "Probably no more room in the sock drawer," I replied.

I found the cord to the coffee maker in the linen closet. (Where else?) Jonathan came over and picked it up.

Melinda came for the typewriter. ("Oh, kid, I almost *died!* We couldn't find it at first. We thought it had been stolen.")

I sat down with a cold beer and the Trib. Pretty soon, I noticed it seemed awfully quiet.

"Where'd Katie go?" I asked.

"Oh, she and Melinda decided it was still so nice outside that they'd ride their bikes over to the park, then go by April's to study."

I said: "How come there's a typewriter in the middle of the living room floor?"

Robin Bred Rest

Some signs of spring around here. A sliver of sunlight slipped through the gray skies, and hung over the city like a pale slice of lemon.

There is snow in the Sierra, and most of the rest of the country is clutched tightly by winter. But Southern California has hummingbirds right now.

We got a hummingbird feeder as a Christmas gift from the neighbors.

"Hang it high, so the cats can't get to the birds," I was advised.

Unnecessary advice. My cats would not know what to do with anything that did not come out of a can.

They are like laboratory mice. Their appetites are triggered by the sound of the electric can-opener.

(Rover—the cat—at one time did get wild enough to go smell a lizard. The lizard bit him. At that very moment, Rover learned how to climb a tree.)

I figure the hummingbirds could hum in my cats' ears and be perfectly safe.

I haven't seen any robins yet. They are probably still sunning in Acapulco.

Robins wait until the pyracantha berries bloom and drop to the ground before they return.

The berries, after a day or two on the ground, distill into an alcohol as powerful as Old Throat-Clutcher.

The robin eats the berries and gets drunk as a lord.

Then he staggers around on the ground, bumping into other robins. Those that can get airbone usually fly sideways, with a little dipsy-doodle now and then.

But don't look for robins until the berries drop.

No use going into town before the bar opens.

Step to the Back of the Bus

Sunny mornings on the J Street Line. I drive a couple of school bus runs every morning during the week. The PS Express to four different schools.

(P.S.—FIVE different schools on rainy days, including the close one just up the street.)

I have seen that smiling bus driver on the TV commercial. The one that says: ". . . and leave the driving to *us*."

I don't know why he's smiling. I'm not smiling. (And I would be perfectly happy to leave the driving to him, if I could figure it out.)

On second thought, I *do* know why he's smiling.

He's smiling because he does not have to go into the bedrooms every morning and roust out his passengers to make his schedule. ("C'mon, c'mon! Everybody's going to be late!")

He's smiling because he does not have to bring in all the half-filled coffee cups from the car after his run.

He's smiling because he feels good. He looks shaved, showered, and fresh as a daisy. (He probably filmed that thing in the early afternoon, after a two-martini lunch.)

I have to pull up at the first school at 7:30 a.m. I wake up at 7 a.m. You can figure out what I look like. All whiskers and sleep in the eyes.

The first trip is the high school run. I honestly do not know who all I carry on this run. I know the names of three or four, but there are always a few extra from around the neighborhood.

"Morning," they say. "Morning," I say. "Step to the rear of the bus, please."

We usually have two or three false starts before we get into gear. "Wait! Wait! I have to go back in and get my homework!" Or: "Hey, my lunch! I forgot my lunch!"

We also have the "Exact Change" rule on our line. Only I am the one who has to come up with the exact change. A quarter to everybody to ride the city bus home.

It's worth it.

The second run is the Roosevelt Junior High and Texas Street Nursery School special. The nursery school chick rides shotgun with me.

(Between runs I have a coffee break, lasting sometimes up to five minutes.)

On this one, we also pick up a few strays. This run carries mostly females, and it's a pretty talky ride.

(They've got all kinds of things to tell each other, because they haven't had a chance to talk since last night on the phone.)

The last passenger is the nursery school one. She is wound up tight as a bedspring in the early morning. Wide awake and bright as a new penny.

Her mind spins through a dozen different subjects on that last mile. "I know how flowers grow. You just put water on 'em and they grow. Avalanches are bad, aren't they? What comes after Q?"

Then I return to the empty house, fill my empty coffee cup, put a piece of blank paper in the typewriter and stare at it blankly. It stares back at me the same way.

Spring Is When You're Ready for It

Gray, gloomy days around here. (I write that because Nature likes to dispute me. And I could use some sunshine.)

However, with spring in my heart, I went out and bought a new barbecue. Naturally, it came in a lot of little pieces to be put together.

"The instructions are simple," said the salesman. "Any child could put it together." Childishly, I believed him.

The picture showed that the thing, when put together, was a sophisticated piece of equipment. A top on it with movable vents. An ash catching tray. A heat indicator.

The simple instructions seemed complicated to me.

"Attach O bolt to L at point where Z tag meets M . . ." So I took the salesman at his word, and turned the whole thing over to a child. (A child who has taken metal shop.)

He put it together without the instructions. "I just looked at the picture," he said. "It was easy."

(The kid was born with screwdrivers for fingers. And he likes to rub it in.)

I said: "That's the way I was going to do it, but I had to run to the store."

He gave me a sad, skeptical smile.

The wife came home and stepped out into the back yard. It was nearly dusk. "What are you doing?" she asked.

I said: "Stoking up my new barbecue. How do you like it?"

She said: "You're going to barbecue? In the middle of winter?"

I said: "What are you talking about? It's February, isn't it? This is San Diego, isn't it?"

She said: "How come you're wearing your mackinaw and gloves?"

I said: "So I won't burn myself lifting the grill. Do you want me to fix dinner or not? Why don't you just go mix a drink."

She said: "I'd better make you a hot toddy. You're blue."

I couldn't find a recipe for barbecuing three whole chickens, so I made one up. I placed each chicken on a big square of foil and put 10 or 15 cloves of garlic around it.

"You've been watching the Galloping Gourmet again," she said. "Here's your toddy. Maybe you'll stop shivvering."

I salted and peppered the birds, poured a little sweet-and-sour sauce over them, and wrapped strips of bacon like a sash across their breasts.

Then I poured a splash of cold Chablis over each one and sealed them up in the foil. "An old Boy Scout trick," I said.

She said: "You carried Chablis as a Boy Scout?" I said: "Up north, where I did my scouting, the mountain streams were the same as chilled white wine."

I let the birds cook over the grill in the foil for about half an hour, then I peeled off all the junk so they could brown.

About an hour after I had started, a neighbor came running through the back gate. "What's wrong?" he said. "I saw smoke pouring out of your backyard!"

I said: "Calm down and have a toddy."

He said: "Thanks, I could use one. It's freezing. Say, you aren't . . . yes, you are. Aren't you?"

I don't know what happened to all the other pioneers. I guess they pulled up stakes and moved west.

Love and Lace Paper

Since we are coming up on Valentine's Day pretty fast, may I be permitted a few words on the subject of love today? Permission granted. (It's nice to be in charge.)

Love, as you know, makes the world go around. Love also makes me go around. As far as I can recall, I have been going around it since my own days of knee pants and peanut butter sandwiches.

Also, I have been associating pretty closely for some years with several members of a younger generation who are constantly in love.

When they are not in love with somebody specific, they are in love with love.

And when they *are* in love with somebody specific, it is mighty difficult to get to use the telephone.

(Although, I have noticed they do not really talk too much on the phone. They mostly just sit there and listen to each other breathe.)

It is practically as contagious as the chickenpox.

Right now I would guess five or six members of this family are in love. And several others appear to be on the verge.

The littlest moppet is in love with *everybody*. She said: "You should love everybody, huh?" She has learned this sound philosophy at nursery school.

Therefore, I suppose everybody in the class must get a valentine from everybody else. In fact, I understand that is the way in other lower grades these days.

I guess it promotes democracy, but what about romance?

Not so when I was snipping red hearts and pasting them onto lacy doilies. In those days, I gave one big valentine to one person. Maybe a couple of so-so valentines to a couple of so-so friends.

Boys would not be caught dead giving valentines to other boys. (Girls gave valentines to everybody. But you know girls.)

We did give valentines to Sister Philomena. (Sister Phil, we called her. But not to her face. She wielded a mean ruler.) Then she would tell us a story about good St. Valentine.

Well, it has come to my attention—and been properly filed—that there were *two* St. Valentines, and neither one of them has a blessed thing to do with Valentine's Day.

Fact of the matter is, it is actually a carryover from what used to be a sort of Roman festival. (Which is not quite as bad as a pagan festival, but bad enough.)

The Roman festival was called Lupercalia, and it honored Juno, the Roman goddess of marriage, and Pan, the god of nature. And from what I read, the Romans closed the banks on that day, and a lot of hi-de-ho took place in the streets.

As the day came down through the years, it became even more curious.

It reached a point at one time in England, where young ladies would slap themselves on the forehead with a rose petal.

If the petal broke, the girl knew her valentine loved her. (If not, she settled for a headache.)

Well, love has led me down many paths over the years. (And given me a few headaches along the way.)

Now, I find myself starting all over right at the beginning. Pasting up valentines for this moppet with cake crumbs on her face.

(Here's one with a bear holding a heart. "I can't bear it if you won't be my valentine.")

I said: "I'll paste them up for you, but you have to travel the rest of the road yourself. And it's a long, long trail."

Sidney's Lady

Under a great deal of pressure from a lot of wailing moppets, I went out the other afternoon and purchased a bird.

"Sidney's lonesome!" they moaned. Sidney being the bright green parakeet who lives in the cage in the utility room.

I said: "How do you know Sidney is lonesome? I've never heard a word of complaint from him. In fact, he rarely says anything. Just sits around, muttering to himself and keeping an eye on the cats."

They said: "The reason he doesn't sing is, he's lonesome!"

I doubt it. I believe the reason he doesn't sing is, when he does, the cats start keeping an eye on *him.*

However, nothing would do but to buzz down to the local pet shop and pick up a powder blue, $5.98, parakeet.

"Is it a girl parakeet?" they demanded.

I said: "I don't know if it's a girl parakeet. I didn't ask for references. For that matter, we don't even know if Sidney is a boy parakeet. Let's let them thrash it out. It's a parakeet, at least. All Sidney's had up to now is a mirror."

I highly suspect the blue parakeet is a female. For one thing, it has such a feminine color. A blue as pale as a prom gown.

For another thing, it has not stopped talking since it arrived. And I have noticed Sidney just sits there, clenching his knuckles and nodding his head.

All this commotion in the bird cage has aroused considerable interest among the three cats. To the point, in fact, that they have quit sleeping on the hamster cage and spend most of their time in the utility room.

Gazing upward—and looking. And thinking.

The new bird does not look like a girl parakeet to them. Or a boy parakeet, for that matter.

To the cats, it looks like a Colonel Sander's chicken. Paw-lickin' good.

"Will we have baby parakeets?" they all asked.

I said: "If that bird does not learn to keep its mouth shut, we may not have grownup parakeets very long. One of those cats is going to come up with an idea pretty soon."

However, I promised I would get a wooden parakeet nest, and we would give spring a chance.

"It's the only way," I said. "Parakeets will not lay eggs in anything but a wooden, concave nest. No straw or feathers. Just a wooden nest. It looks a little like a soup bowl, and clips onto the side of the cage."

(I got this information once after listening to an incredible lecture from a bird lady about "Daddy Bird's responsibilities in baby-sitting" and "teensie eggs" and how "we mustn't forget that a baby is a baby whether it has skin or feathers.")

They said: "How do you like your new friend, Sidney?"

Sidney looked back and blinked pleadingly, as if to say: "Couldn't you get her to pipe down? Where'd you find this chick, anyway?"

The Man Who Turned His Back

"America has furnished to the world the character of Washington. And if our American institutions had done nothing else, that alone would have entitled them to the respect of mankind."

Daniel Webster said that, and it's worth remembering as we begin this four-day weekend.

Washington's birthday has been switched around by Washington, D.C. It is actually next Tuesday, but we celebrate it on Monday so everybody can have a three-day weekend.

Apparently there's no way to figure out a three-day weekend without packaging the national images of Lincoln and Washington.

Why has there never been an important movie about George Washington? He has been a minor character in a few, but the real man has never been studied on film.

How could you miss with a character who walked coolly away from a soldier who had a musket trained on his back?

George Washington, the father of the country, has remained an unfinished portrait for most of his countrymen.

If you wear false teeth, you may be interested in knowing that George Washington had his first tooth removed when he was 22, but had none of his own after 57.

A Dr. Greenwood, America's first native-born oral surgeon, was Washington's dentist. He supplied the president with several sets of dentures.

These were shaped like rat traps; the springs were so strong that unless Washington kept his jaws clinched, his mouth would fly open.

Dr. Greenwood used hippopotamus tusk as the material for the false teeth, but they turned black in time.

He told Washington it was caused "either by your soaking them in port wine, or by your drinking it."

I visited the Washington Monument on a summer's day. Paid a dime and took the elevator to the top. (It's 555 feet high and 898 steps up, if you want to save the money.)

The afternoon sun cast the shadow of the spire across the east lawn of Potomac Park and over a portion of the folding chairs set up for the outdoor summer Shakespeare festival.

(It seemed ironic. The monument for the man who beat the British, providing shade for England's pride, William Shakespeare.)

George Washington is not buried at the monument. His body rests beside Martha's, a short distance from their home in Mt. Vernon.

But the spirit of the man is felt at the monument. It is tall, stately, seemingly built to last forever.

Across nearby Reflection Pool is the Abraham Lincoln Memorial.

Both monuments shimmer on the surface of the rectangular pond—one to the man who won the Union, the other to the man who saved it.

When the light is just right, the two seem to reach across to each other.

Days like spring and a four-day holiday thrown in. (No one threw a holiday at me, though. And I have utmost regard for Mr. Lincoln and Mr. Washington.)

This past week has been terribly confusing for the muffin in nursery school. They usually draw pictures about the holidays.

She didn't know *what* to draw.

I said: "How about a picture of Lincoln chopping down a Valentine tree?" (I am not really considered much help.)

She settled for making a big Valentine. A red heart on a lacy doily. She gave it to her mother.

"Maybe I'll make you one tomorrow," she said. I shrugged philosophically. "Maybe" is better than nothing.

I sent the wife two Valentines. One was a gag. It said: "I've got half a mind to ask you to be my Valentine."

The inside said: "The other half wants to ask Sophia Loren."

(I am not really considered very funny around here, either.)

In the fury of the first signs of spring, I am likely to go mad and buy wild clothes. Gaudy, wide ties. Flowered shirts, flared pants.

Then I never have the courage to wear them.

I did buy a puffed sleeved shirt that had a million little blue flowers on it. The wife said: "I like it. It makes you look slimmer."

I got home and put it on. It made me look like a meadow. I said: "I can't wear this shirt. It doesn't have a pocket."

It's still hanging in the closet somewhere.

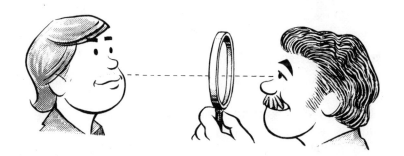

Picnic weather around here. I said: "Let's go to Balboa Park this weekend. Pack up the portable barbecue. Pick up some hamburger. Maybe toss the Frisbie around."

A child said: "Barbecuing is pollution."

This is what they learn in school. Things to come home and bug the outdoor chef with.

I said: "Okay, kid. I will fix up a very special dish for you. Tartar steak. How does that sound?"

He said: "What's Tartar steak?"

I said: "It's a slab of raw hamburger with a sprig of parsley on top."

The sunshine is putting the bloom on everything. The side yard is bursting with camellias. Roses cut back during winter are beginning to sprout little green shoots.

That's not all that's growing.

The 15-year-old boy has decided to grow a moustache. He's been growing it for three days now.

He took me out into the bright sunlight yesterday afternoon so I could see it.

The Old Blue Guitar

Moody skies these days. Wake up with sunshine and bluebirds in your hair. An hour later, you're running for cover.

The household has had some moody moments lately. People a little more jumpy than usual.

I put it down to the approach of spring fever.

"I've noticed it at work, too," said the wife. "It's been days since I've heard much laughter around there. Seems to be a general blue mood going around."

I said: "Maybe I ought to break out the old blue guitar. Whip off a couple of old ballads to cheer everybody up."

> *"O, the val-l-ley was fired at sunrise,*
> *"Just after the break of the da-a-ay.*
> *"And while the echo linger-r-r-ed,*
> *"A soul had passed a-wa-ay."*

She said: "Oh, that's a *great* help. I think I'll go take a hot bath."

"Into the arms of his maker,
"And there to hear his fa-a-a-te.
"A tear, a sigh, a sad goodbye,
"O, the pardon came to la-a-a-te."

I could hear the water running in the bathroom. Running hard and loud.

It's a tense world, friends. Tension causes a lot of troubles— including overweight. (That calming toddy is loaded with calories.)

"Many compulsive eaters are simply trying to settle their nerves. They become tense and reach for the refrigerator." This is the word from a published medic.

He says the nervous eater is likely to pile up a sandwich because it can be made in a hurry.

That figures. The sandwich was invented by a tense man in a hurry.

Lord John Montagu Sandwich was sitting at the gambling table with an extremely hot streak going for him. He was nervous as a cat and didn't want to stop to go eat.

"Just slice me some meat and pheasant, Crumley, and put it between a couple pieces of bread. I'll eat it that way."

Thus, the noble sandwich was born. (Ask your history teacher.)

I do not reach for the refrigerator when I get blue. I reach for somebody else's troubles. A sad book. A sad song.

The trick is, to find somebody in worse shape. Then I feel better.

"There's a memory that lingers in our hearts still,
"And a picture that's turned toward the wall . . ."

I stick to the old, mournful ballads. Things like "Long Black Veil" and "Little Box of Pine."

In Search of the Sea

In search of a little refreshment for the soul, we drove over to Ocean Beach the other afternoon and checked into rooms right on the edge of the crashing sea.

I pulled back the drapes and walked out onto the small balcony.

The Pacific was having this wildly wonderful argument with the wind. Foamy surf splashed right to the top of the municipal pier, and up and over the Mission Bay jettys.

The sea acts like a tranquilizer for my wife and me.

There are other such mental medicants. The smell of pine trees. A spot of warm sunshine anywhere. A clear night sky. Certain books and certain music.

But none is as powerful as the sea, in any mood it happens to be in.

I don't know how I lived so many years without it. And I doubt if I would ever be able to again.

I can't remember exactly when I first saw the ocean. It was one day in Oregon. I was nine, and the son of escapees from the dusts of Oklahoma and Arizona.

But I can remember the feeling. It was gray and deadly looking, pounding on black rocks from the mist.

At the same time, it was wonderful. And I felt all that red dust and gray sand really washed away for the first time.

I lived five years in Oregon, and never saw the sea again during that time. We lived inland, and there were other things to do on our 10-acres besides taking Sunday drives to the coast.

Some years later, I was sent to live with an uncle in Boston, and I got to see the Atlantic. But it wasn't the Atlantic as opposed to the Pacific.

It was simply the sea. The awesome, moody, mind-binding sea.

Later, now in California but still inland, there was the business of growing up to attend to. School, parttime jobs, and football kept me busy. Sacramento was less than 100 miles from the ocean, but I might just as well have lived in Nebraska.

When I joined the Air Force, they sent me back to the dust—to Texas.

After the Air Force, many years afterwards, I was pounding out copy high and dry in the mountains. I had worked 15 years with the same company, had a secure job and future, and life was vaguely smooth.

But I still did not live by the sea.

One day I said to myself: "Dammit, my life is half over, and I want to live by the sea!"

So I quit the job and moved by the sea.

It was that simple, really. And the only regret I've ever had was that I didn't do it sooner.

It's a pity that the edges of all our seas aren't big enough for everybody to live on. And for those who've seen it and don't live there—I don't know how they stand it.

So Much for Poetry

Warm and golden days around here. A clear, clean sky, and the sparkling bay laced with drifting sails.

So much for poetry. The blasted vacuum cleaner broke the other day.

Not exactly true. It did not just stand there in the corner and break. It was broken *by* someone.

I told the moppets a long time ago: "Do *not* ride on the vacuum cleaner. It is not a hobby horse. It might break."

That doesn't mean anything. I have found the average child can look you right in the face, nod at your every word, and not hear a blessed thing you say.

They simply are not tuned in on the same wave length. (I think I could get across to them if I could afford a television commercial. That's where they're tuned in.)

As predicted, the vacuum broke. The handle bone is no longer connected to the sweeper bone.

I said: "Now hear the word of the *lord*! I'm going to take this thing down and get it fixed. And if it is not treated tenderly in the future, somebody may get their tender block knocked off!"

While the vacuum cleaner was in the shop, the dishwasher quit working. These miracle gadgets always go out in a series. I think it's a miracle.

I called the repair man. "We'll be out tomorrow," he said. "Probably in the morning."

Tomorrow came and we waited. In the mid-afternoon, the man still had not showed up.

We left the house for less than 15 minutes. Told the teen-age daughter we'd be right back.

When we came back—you guessed it. The repair man had been there. "He wouldn't come in because there was no adult at home," she said.

I called the shop. "That's our policy," they said.

I said: "Your man would have come into the house if my wife had been here alone, wouldn't he?"

They said: "Certainly."

I said: "Listen, my wife is barely five feet tall. But that girl is nearly as tall as I am, and strong enough to deck any repair man you've got. Besides that, I think she knows karate."

The garbage disposal jammed. I said: "You simply *cannot* dispose of teaspoons in the garbage disposal."

The child said: "Sorry." I said: "Sorry for what?" He said: "For what you said." I said: "What did I say?" He said: "Huh?" (See what I mean?)

I called the shop. The *same* shop I talked to before. They said there would be a service call charge for the disposal *and* the dishwasher.

I said: "Can't your man fix them in the same trip?"

They said: "The man who repairs dishwashers is not the man who repairs disposals."

It's the age of specialists.

"Never mind!" yelled the wife, "I got it unstuck with a broom handle."

One of the younger children came in. "Could you see what's wrong with the TV?"

An older boy came in with another problem. "How come we only get static on the car radio?"

Warm and golden days around here. A clear, clean sky, and the sparkling bay laced with drifting sails. (I think I may go jump in the sparkling bay laced with drifting sails.)

Reserve for Small Boys

March winds slipping through our canyons. Spring kites dancing high over our green hills. (Dancing the bump in the fickle breeze.)

> *"And the spring arose on the garden fair,*
> *"Like the spirit of love felt everywhere;*
> *"And each flower and herb on earth's dark breast*
> *"Rose from the dreams of its wintry rest."*

Percy Shelley wrote that about March. A pretty heavy writer, that Percy. (He had to be with a first name like that, a weird friend like Lord Byron and a wife who wrote "Frankenstein.")

It is the time of the year when all the neighborhood dogs and small boys disappear. Like the March winds, they are slipping through our canyons. Leading expeditions against Indian war parties, camping with Robin Hood under a green cover, sniffing out the hidden homes of gophers and skunks.

We have a beautiful canyon near our house. Every day at dusk, the boys and dogs pour out of it like factory workers at the 5 o'clock whistle.

Home to the television, the dinner, the evening of the day.

I never had such canyons as a boy, but I had a hill that was about as good.

On one side of the hill there were trees, thickets, scooped-out brush caves, and beds of rich green and soft moss.

It was a place to spend hours and hours of the day. A place to read, to think, to run, to doze in the summer sun.

On the other side of the hill was an ancient graveyard. I also spent many hours on that side, walking among the old names and old dates. (But I sure never slept on that side of the hill.)

But our canyons here are special things. A touch of real wilderness smack in the middle of one of the largest cities in the nation.

Before somebody finds a way to make a dollar out of messing them up, maybe they should be designated as Natural Wilderness Areas—dedicated to small boys, dogs, gophers, skunks, and birds.

Gourmets in the Sand

Summer-like days and low low tides in the afternoon. We drove to La Jolla, set up for the afternoon in a small cove south of *the* Cove, and I went exploring tidepools.

I used to know the names of everything in these pools—even the Latin names of the seaweed. (I majored in marine biology, but it's been a long long time.)

Still, it's fascinating to hunch down and look into those private little worlds. The anemones. The purple pin-cushion urchins. Hermit crabs. Rock crabs. Plankton.

The vast majority of sea life—I seem to recall a figure like 80 or 90 percent—lives within 250 yards of the shoreline. An average tidepool has a population as big as San Diego's.

No population problems in a tidepool, though. They have a built-in solution. Everybody just keeps eating everybody else.

It's a busy sea-food restaurant, open 24 hours a day.

On shore, a bunch of seagulls had landed and were attending a class. At least that's what we call it—Sea Gull School.

All the birds but one stand facing the same direction. That one bird is out in front of the group and facing them. He looks for all the world like a teacher. Sea Gull School.

We spread our blanket against a cliff wall, laid out sun lotion, a portable barbecue grill, and a couple books that I never got around to opening.

Instead, I took a length of fishline and spent a couple of hours stringing a shell necklace for my wife.

I said: "You know something? I'm really enjoying this."

She said: "Stringing beads has always been a pretty well known therapy."

I guess that must have been it.

About 4 o'clock it was time to play my game. It's called "How To Thoroughly Enjoy The Beach And At The Same Time Make Everbody Else There Hate You." I get some kind of fiendish delight in it.

First, I fired up the barbecue. Then my wife cut up some zuccini and wrapped it in foil with a slice of cheese and a wedge of butter.

Next, I pulled out a small loaf of sour French bread. (People were already beginning to eye us.)

When the coals were hot, we put the zuccini on the grill. Then, I reached into the ice chest and took out two beautiful steaks.

As soon as they hit the grill, the flavor began drifting all around the beach. Everybody around us was looking now. (I have never seen so many faces of starvation.)

Now that I had everybody's attention, I reached into the ice chest and pulled out the topper—a chilled magnum of champagne and two long-stemmed glasses.

(One guy looked at the beer in his hand, poured out what was left in disgust on the sand, and got up and left.)

Before we were halfway through with our dinner (on a white tablecloth, I should add), there wasn't another person left on our section of the beach.

Only the seagulls were left to watch me enjoy the brandy and cigar.

Saga of Johnny Mintseed

Spring is rushing in on us. It is on the hillsides, in the green canyons, in the backyard, in our hearts.

Tomorrow is Arbor Day in some places. Plant a tree, people. You'll feel better.

Aldo Leopold, the conservationist and author, said it eloquently:

"Acts of creation are ordinarily reserved for gods and poets, but humbler folk may circumvent this restriction if they know how. To plant a pine, for example, one need be neither god nor poet; one need only own a shovel. By virtue of this curious loophole in the rules, any clodhopper may say: 'Let there be a tree—and there will be one.' "

I think I may be such a clodhopper. When I was about 10, I read the story of Johnny Appleseed. Then, as I did with most stories I read at that age, I played the part.

I ate so many green apples, I got sick. But I went up on a gentle hillside near Eugene, Ore., and planted all the cores.

There's no way of knowing whether any apple trees grew. I don't think I could even find that hill again. It may be a subdivision or a shopping center by now.

But I hope not.

There is no room left in this yard to plant a tree, but I may plant a few clumps of mint under the faucet. I think I know where I can get some julep to mix with it.

I will plant the little shoots under the faucet, and turn the handle so I get a slight but constant drip. Then I will say: "Let there be mint"—and there will be.

Just call me Johnny Mintseed.

During the long, warm summer, I will sit in the courtyard, sipping mint juleps and listening to the Padres. Maybe I will break out the old blue guitar and strum a little between innings.

If anyone approaches me with clever ideas about putting up the screens or taking out the carpets, I will patiently explain that I am occupied as a conservationist.

And if they care to know what I am conserving, I will say: "Myself."

Up with the chattering birds these spring mornings. I put the kettle on the instant heat burner. For instant coffee. Mixed myself an instant breakfast. Shaved with instant foam.

I yelled from the bathoom: "I can't *stand* this instant jazz much longer! I may move west."

An idle threat. How can you move west when you've only got a couple of miles of west left?

Still, I feel a little like an electric watch. Plugged in and self-winding. And wound up about tight enough to spring loose.

We have been shopping around for a retreat. A place away from people and places.

I check the ads in the paper. I said: "Here's something. Twenty acres with a trout stream, trees and deer, only $350 an acre."

She said: "Where is it?"

I said: "Someplace in Utah. It doesn't say."

She said: "That's silly. How would we get there and back in a weekend?"

I said: "We can spend the whole weekend getting there. Who's coming back?"

The Fish That Stands on Its Tail

A warm night. The moon sparkled on the waves like flecks from a spinning ballroom reflector. We walked along the midnight shore in search of the elusive grunion.

I have no doubt there *is* such a fish as the grunion. I have heard about them for years. I even have a picture of some in a biology textbook.

Leuresthes tenuis, a smeltlike fish about six inches long—the grunion.

But I have never seen a grunion. And I have been looking for a long time.

"They're great seafood. I've roasted hundreds over an open beach fire." An outdoor writer told me that. A man I feel I can trust. (But then, I've never *seen* him eat a grunion, either.)

I'm not sure I want to eat a grunion. Or even catch one. I just want to look at one.

They are weird creatures, I understand, and weird creatures are part of my stock in trade.

Well, in case you don't know it, I will give you the life story of the grunion—based entirely on second hand facts, I must add.

Grunion, This Is Your Life:

The delicious little grunion swims around in the sea, minding his own business and trying to stay away from bigger fish, until spring. Then the grunion, boys and girls alike, get moonstruck.

At this point, he does an odd thing for a fish to do. He (and she) comes ashore, and they do a love dance on their tails.

The grunion's timing is as accurate as a Navy clock. (And outdoor writers know these times and tell their readers about them, and everybody goes down to the beach and scoops up hundreds of grunion. HAH!)

During the months of March, April, May and June, on the second, third, and fourth nights after the full moon, the boy grunion tells the girl grunion: "Take my hand, baby, and let's go for a stroll on the beach."

The grunion comes in just after the high spring tide has turned, and I don't expect it is necessary to point out exactly what happens next.

However, it is at this moment that Southern Californians lined up along the beaches, run down and scoop up the fish in hands, pails, hats, or whatever. (I imagine the grunion must feel a little like they're being raided.)

The late Max Miller of La Jolla liked the grunion, disliked the people who took them, and wrote some words about it:

"On grunion-run night the beach is not the lonely beach of most nights. Instead, the sands are illuminated by fires each few yards.

"People by the dozens have arrived to turn the ocean, my ocean, into theatricals. And if I had the power to call out to the grunion not to come ashore on these nights I would do so. I would call as loudly as I could.

"And on some other night, when the people were all gone, I would whisper to the grunion: 'It's all right now. You may come in.' "

I've got an idea the spirit of Max Miller walks with me when I trod the sands of La Jolla Shores in search of the grunion.

And Max must have the power by now.

Sometimes a Swallow

Mission San Juan Capistrano sits close to the sea in a sheltered valley, where wild grapes once grew as thickly as in a vineyard. Tomorrow is St. Joseph's Day. Tomorrow the swallows are due to return.

Progress has sinned against the once beautiful setting—the seventh mission of Father Junipero Serra.

Now it is hemmed in by refreshment stands, gas stations, and curio shops where you can buy a swallow on a T-shirt, an ash tray, a cheap necklace, or a postcard.

What's more, the swallows don't come en masse on St. Joseph's day. They begin dribbling in during the first really warm days of March. But if you ask a local merchant about the birds already flitting around in the trees of the Mission grounds, he will tell you they are sparrows.

On the 19th, the sparrows turn into swallows, and the legend lives on.

Gone now are the Indians, the sprawling Mission cattle land, and the once most splendid church of California. The little padre himself, who limped across California three times, is buried under the altar of his Mission in Carmel.

Still there were days—long, long ago.

Flowers in the Plumbing

The youngest moppet is out picking flowers these afternoons. She said: "See what I picked for you and Mommy?" Mommy said: "Oh, thank you, honey."

I said: "You know something? We don't *have* any flowers like that in *our* yard." (Uh Oh!)

When there is nobody around to give the flowers to, she puts them in water.

It's a problem, though. For she cannot reach the taps on the kitchen sink.

However, she can reach everything that holds water in the bathroom. She puts flowers in the sink. Flowers in the bathtub. Flowers in the —well, everywhere!

I tell you, it makes you feel a little like a royal guest at a South Seas resort hotel when you find flower petals floating in your . . . your—well, *every*where!

We are coming up on the National Daffodil Festival in a few days.

We are prepared.

Spring will take two days to begin in the United States this year. It starts Sunday at 1:38 a.m. on the East Coast. Since there's a three hour time difference, we can start living spring up here tomorrow night.

(Talk about editorial research.)

The two spring kittens' eyes are open. I don't know if they can really see, but they're open.

(For years I've been writing "blue as a kitten's eyes." Not much editorial research there. Kittens' eyes are black.)

I picked up one kitten and it squealed like a banshee. The mother cat came bounding into the room, gave me a dirty look, and walked in circles around my legs. As if to say: "What do *you* know about kittens. Put my child *down*!"

This is the same ungrateful cat I fed for weeks with a doll's baby bottle after her mother was lost.

Now, she looks on me as sort of a nosy grandparent. Not really up on child care.

I said: "Look, cat, this is not really your nursery. It is *my* closet.

I was merely picking up your kid so I could look for a sock."

Flowers in the plumbing, kittens in the closet, and the sounds of spring cleaning through the rest of the house.

She said: "There's no reason for the house to be messy with this many teen-agers around." Then she sat down and spent two days making up a chart of rotating duties for every day of the month.

The chart was announced at the evening meal. (The applause was scant, let me tell you.)

"On some days," she said, "you may have two jobs. But on other days, you may have no job at all."

(The moppets are all in favor of "other days.")

The chart works fairly well. (The dishes and pans get put in different places every night, but you can't expect perfection.)

There are some minor outbreaks.

"You didn't wash those three pans."

"They weren't mine. They were left from the day before."

The one with the duty the day before said he ran out of hot water because somebody else took a shower too long.

I went into the bathroom, looked at all the pretty floating flowers, and dreamed dreams of the South Seas.

Love and Teeth

Spring fever gripped the household. Fevers ran about 101. Scratchy throats, coughs and colds. Days of wine-red noses.

When everybody got well, I spent half the morning writing notes.

I see science also has spring fever. They are messing around with matters romantic again. Exploring the subject of tender love with federal funds.

Here are two Japanese medics who have discovered the kissprint.

They say lip prints are just as individual as fingerprints. The only difference is, the lip prints are likely to change with age.

However, it is a matter of record that a Los Angeles police lieutenant solved a hit-run case when he found the victim's lip prints on the suspected car.

Next time you get hit by a car, try to kiss it before it gets away.

A Michigan doctor reports his research shows girls in love are healthier than girls who aren't. Co-eds all tangled up in moonlight and roses have less colds than the others.

Also, girls with boyfriends have healthier teeth, he said.

(I told the wife: "Let her stay on the phone. We have enough dental bills around here.")

Science also tells us today that many husbands are more interested in the aromas of food than perfumes. "A wife might command quicker attention from her mate if she smelled more like fresh bread or peppermint than one of the expensive perfumes," they said.

Grandma could have told science that. She never let any of her daughters wear lipstick, perfume or makeup to the box socials.

She said: "A pinch of the cheeks and a dab of vanilla extract is all you need."

I do not have scientific research to back it up, but I predict it will be a warm spring with a good deal of this love thing going round.

I predict a lot of cupcakes who are trembling on the brink of decision will be saying "I do" before summer begins. This will undoubtedly cost fathers a lot in wedding feathers, but it may save on the dental bills.

"Marriage is on its way out as an institution," I read in one scientific journal (and a *lot* of current magazines). But there's still a line every day at the county clerk's desk.

(For what it's worth, I also predict that as long as we have marriage, we will have institutions.)

Science, turning from Michigan co-eds and the powers of perfume, has a romantic pronouncement on the lonesome oyster.

"The Atlantic Coast oysters remain either male or female all their lives. But Pacific Coast oysters are all mixed up and switch from male to female and back about every five years."

I don't know if this is just a scientific oddity, or a statement of the way things are out here on the West Coast.

"Do I smell the toast burning, or is that your comb?"

I said: "What kind of dialogue is that to toss at a man who is just out of his sick bed?"

Marry a strange woman and you get a lot of strange questions.

She said: "I *meant* your hot comb! I thought I smelled something burning, then I saw you were using your new comb."

(I looked in the mirror. My hair wasn't on fire.)

I said: "You'd better check the toast."

Sunny days. The bluebird of health landed briefly on our rooftop, allowing everybody in the household to go back to school and work for the first time in two weeks.

I said: "Now everybody stay away from people with germs. I don't want a new cycle of this started around here."

They said: "What about when we're in the classroom?"

I said: "Don't breathe when you're in the classroom. Stay healthy."

One eye on the bluebird, the other on the thermometer.

Chilly evenings, but it's warm in our heart. We moved the barbecue onto the veranda so we can make burnt offerings all year long.

(I imagine it boggles the neighbors to look across the canyon on a rainy day and see me flipping hamburgers. But I don't get a chance to make many other waves.)

We use the inside range, too, but it bugs us a little bit. I think it is haunted.

You see, we cannot turn the overhead fan off. It is supposed to turn off automatically when you slide the hood in. But it does not.

However, it does turn off if you walk away from the stove.

Step back to within three feet of it, and it turns back on. Weird, but the gospel truth.

Other mechanical things around here also work in strange ways. The toast is supposed to go down automatically when you put it in the toaster.

It doesn't.

Except when the smallest boy puts toast in it. Then the toaster works perfectly. Slips right down and begins turning a toasty brown.

Now, I have stood and watched him put the toast in. We *all* have watched him. He doesn't seem to put it in any differently.

However, we try to do it exactly as he does. Nothing.

"Here," he says, "let me do it." And the toast goes down. The boy with the magic touch.

Another thing. I am the *only* one who can work the can opener around here. Nobody else can get it to work.

But, I understand from some of my friends, that's not too unusual. None of their wives can open cans, either.

(When I get to feeling better, maybe I will try to figure some of these things out.)

I Kept Falling Uphill

Plenty of snow at the big Sierra resorts these days. Skiers are filling the lifts at Squaw Valley, Dodge Ridge, Mammoth, Mount Rose.

I used to be a skiing writer. However, I did not report my copy from first-hand observation. You could not get me on skis.

I merely stood at the bottom of the hill and tallied up the statistics. Adding up the casualty count for the day.

In this way, I avoided breaking any of my own bones. But I picked up the lingo of the slopes.

Then, in the evening, I could sit around the roaring fire in the lodge and talk skiing like a man.

I would say things like: "Did you catch the ice on that north slope today? Man, that was like flying on greased glass."

Notice, I did not say that I had *tried* the icy slope. It was a little play on words.

But people looked at me impressed.

Once I tried skiing on the bunny slopes. This is the one where they put 5-year-olds and invalids.

First, I bought one of those stocking caps that completely covered my face. There were little eye holes, and a place for the nose to stick out.

It wasn't that cold, but I didn't want to be recognized.

You don't get a chair-lift on the bunny hill. All you get is a little rope tow—a moving rope that pulls you up about 50 feet to a small slope.

Well, I should have known what kind of trouble was in store for me when I grabbed the rope and fell going *up*hill.

Once at the top, I somehow (and don't ask me how, for I've blotted it from my memory) managed to get into a well-worn path that resembled a bobsled run—but straight down!

I had hardly reached 50 miles an hour before I remembered what I had forgotten. I had forgotten to ask anybody how to stop.

"You should have tried new snow instead of that track," said the nice lady in the Red Cross station.

She said: "Now that you're awake, I'll fill out this report, Name please?"

I said: "John Smith."

The next season I was fortunate enough to break my ankle.

Not skiing, heaven forbid! I broke it in a slight fall from a ladder while painting our mountain cabin.

Well, as soon as I got the cast on, I headed for the slopes. Put on my ski sweater, a stocking cap and a brave smile.

There is no better piece of equipment to take skiing than a cast on your leg. It is an immediate status symbol.

People wrote their names on it. They bought the hot buttered rums, and fetched them from the bar so I would not have to get up.

We sat and talked skiing around the fire through the long evenings, and you would not believe some of the yarns that were spun.

It was my most successful skiing season.

'Dammit Sidney, Make a Noise'

Warm afternoons around here lately. I took a slight snooze in the back yard yesterday afternoon. Then, was slightly awakened by something chewing on my foot.

This would be Sidney, the new lab puppy a son is boarding here. I said: "Cut that out, you blasted cannibal."

Sympathetic letters have been pouring in on how to handle puppies.

"You say he is afraid to be alone. Well, put a piece of your own old clothing in a box for him to sleep on. Add a ticking alarm clock, and a hot water bottle."

I tried the hot water bottle. He chewed it to pieces, and looked up soaked, but grinning.

As for the ticking alarm clock, he does not need it. He sleeps in the den. And somebody is always leaving the television set on all night.

Why give him an alarm clock for company, when he can watch late, late movies all night long?

Still, he will not go to sleep unless somebody is sleeping in the den with him.

Preferably somebody he can chew on now and then.

The second day we had Sidney, I put him outside. I said: "Now, you only have three things to learn right now. First, you are a dog. Second, your name is Sidney. Third, the reason you are outside is now being mopped up in the hallway."

Then I latched the swinging cat door so he could not get back in.

Well, you would have thought he was being tortured on the rack. You have never heard such crying and moaning and scratching.

It was like: "Man, I'm *dying* out here all alone! What am I supposed to do *alone*? It's lonely out here. Where *is* everybody?"

This went on for nearly an hour. Then the wife said: "Where *is* Sidney? I can hear him crying, but he's not outside."

Somehow, he had managed to get through a small hole and get trapped underneath the house.

Naturally, we do not have a flashlight. (I could buy a flashlight every Monday and we would not have one by Friday.)

We rigged up an extension cord and light bulb and I tried to pinpoint where the crybaby was hiding.

His cries seemed to be coming from under a pile of old lumber and an abandoned airconditioner.

I said: "Get me the hammer. I'll have to pry some boards loose to get under there." (I was all dressed for the office, naturally.)

The wife said: "I don't hear him crying anymore. You don't suppose he's dead."

I said: "I don't think so. Sidney! Dammit, Sidney, make a noise so I can hear you."

I crawled through the dust and gunk, threw boards aside, and finally lifted up the old airconditioner.

There he was, down in a pile of dust, looking up, wagging his tail. ("Hi! Here I am. Where you been?")

The dog naturally did not cry while I was looking for him. He could hear boards being flung this way and that, hear me softly calling him some rather strong adjectives.

Why should he have cried at that point? He knew he was no longer alone.

I took him into the house. He drank a bowl of water. Slurp. Then he fell asleep.

The Snaggle-Toothed Crisis

A small crisis came rapping softly on the bedroom door shortly before sunrise. I got up, put on my robe, and stumbled sleepily over to answer it.

The youngest of our brood stood there in pajamas and disbelief. No tears or trembling lips. Just a small expression of hurt shock.

I said: "What is it, honey?"

She said, almost too softly to hear: "The tooth fairy didn't come."

Clang! Clang! Clang! Clang!

My wife, half asleep but with a built-in mother's sound system, *leaped* out of bed, fully awake now, and began stammering:

"Uh . . . ah . . . honey, why don't you . . . uh . . . go back to bed for awhile. The tooth fairy probably hasn't come yet. He doesn't come until . . . until after . . . ('Psst! What time is it?' 'About five-thirty.') . . . until after *six o'clock* sometimes."

She said: "But I can't go back to sleep now."

My wife said: "Well, why don't you go downstairs and play for awhile. Maybe the tooth fairy will come while you're down there."

The moppet left, not so sure of this idea. My wife looked at me with a face full of despair.

I said: "Tooth fairy speak with forked tongue, but talk pretty fast."

I mean, this time the tooth fairy had really botched it up. This time there were *two* teeth to be picked up and pawned. And one of them wasn't even loose! It just had to be taken out to make room for others.

She said: "Good Lord! All the change is downstairs. I left it down there so the kids could pick up their bus fare for school. She's probably playing at the table where I left it."

I said: "Well, go down there and do a little sleight-of-hand, or you'll have to turn in your wings."

She said: "I'm a failure."

It sort of got straightened out, and it sort of didn't. She got her hands on a little change, slipped it in the tooth envelope under the pillow and came back to bed.

Knock, knock, knock. "Come in, honey."

She said: "I got dimes, but I know who the tooth fairy is. It's really your mother. But you're kind of like a fairy, huh?"

Her mother, refusing to cop a plea yet, said: "Really? That's interesting."

She said: "I think so, anyway."

But she didn't think so. Or didn't want to, at least. She would have much preferred to hang on to the belief a little longer, and would gladly have given those two dimes in her hand for a tiny bit of faith.

After all, it was Santa Claus last year, and ghosts and witches the Halloween before. The tooth fairy was about the only old buddy left among that special gang of children's friends. And she still has lots of teeth yet to go.

However, about two hours later, at breakfast, she said: "You know, I did see something look like it went into the clouds this morning. It *could* have been the tooth fairy. Maybe he was late because a lot of children lost their teeth yesterday."

And she smiled a kind of snaggle-tooth smile.

A Man I Once Knew

I knew the man briefly as a boy, and, if I remember correctly, I liked him.

We were friends in Phoenix, Ariz., and I vaguely recall him

taking me rabbit hunting one afternoon. I was too young to shoot, but he carried a bone-handled .44-caliber pistol and shot rabbits from the hip. He hit them, too, and I can remember being pretty impressed.

My other recollections about him are misty. He saved coins; I knew that. He once gave me a Stone Mountain half-dollar.

I also knew he was in the restaurant business. He was a chef, I believe.

And there was a thing he could do with his eyes that I've never seen since. He could make them shiver.

You could get close to his face, look right into his eyes, and he'd make them dance at high-speed from side to side. I've never heard of anybody since who could do that.

One day, when I was 12, he moved out of town. And that was the last I saw of him.

Of course, my impressions were those gathered by a child's mind. We lived in different worlds, and I never really ever knew the adult man.

I heard about him later on. Some other adults I knew said he wasn't the most responsible person in the world. He gambled, I heard, and he drank quite a bit. "He always had to buy three rounds to everybody else's one," a mutual acquaintance told me.

I guess it was so.

His family life, I heard, suffered for this. His first wife divorced him, and he married again at least once. Maybe more often than that.

I heard he had drifted out and back into the restaurant business, from fry-cook to owner. Somebody once told me he was in the used car business, and then I heard he was managing a bowling alley and pool hall somewhere in the midwest.

I also heard he nearly died once. A stroke of some kind, or a heart attack, I believe.

The other day I got a message from him. Twenty-seven years later.

It was a phone call from Los Angeles. He was in California for a short time, and would like to drive down and see me for an hour or two.

I shrugged and said "Sure." It seemed a little awkward, though, I mean, 27 years is a long time. And I never really knew him that well in the first place. Just a brief acquaintance.

But he said that's what he wanted. He said he'd heard that I had children, and he'd like to see some of them if possible.

"Come ahead," I said.

Last Sunday afternoon I was sitting in the kitchen over a cup of coffee when I saw him approach cautiously up the front walkway. I'm surprised I recognized him, but I did.

There he was. An old man with a hunch to his shoulders, a lot of bad road written on his face, but still with a touch of his own brand of style. A diamond ring on his finger, an expensive brown suit and a silk shirt, and a $50 white Stetson hat.

I didn't know whether to laugh or cry. And I sure as hell didn't know what to say to him. So I just opened the front door and said the first thing that came into my mind.

I said: "Hi Dad."

PART TWO

This is Part Two.

Simply a Californian

BODEGA BAY — Fierce winds whipped the gnarled trees of the coastline as we pulled into Wright's Beach Campground here. The surf stood on end, 10 feet tall, just before it pitched over and slapped the sand.

I pulled our borrowed camper into space No. 29, turned off the key, and sat there silently aching for a moment. Driving a camper in the wind all morning is like wrestling somebody bigger than yourself for several hours.

I felt pinned.

However, we had once again taken an inventory on our state. Once again, I felt like a Californian. Not a Southern Californian. No longer a Northern Californian. Simply a Californian.

The Golden State. The Sunshine State. El Dorado. These all fit, but none of them encompass. There is no single word to sum up the land named for the Amazon Goddess Califia.

It is the blue and green beauty of San Diego, where it all began. It is the hurriedness of proud old Los Angeles, where the money rolls in, and the bad breath of industry stings your eyes.

It is stately San Francisco, the grand dame city, so smug with her blueblood lines that she would fool you completely—if you hadn't caught her telling so many blue jokes.

It is an apple stand in Julian, a grain silo in Gridley, a giant stucco orange on Highway 99, a thousand students on the sidewalks of Bancroft Way in Berkeley.

And more, more, more.

Freeways have almost stolen the identities of California's cities, big and small. Now you rarely go through a town. You go over it, or around it. And the concrete ribbon is the same in Sacramento as it is in Petaluma. It has no personality.

Once, when they would do, we had smaller and simpler highways. They were dotted throughout the state with historical markers. "Here, at this spot, on a certain date, a certain thing happened."

You could pull over, park your car, and learn something.

Today, on most of California's highways, if you pull over and park your car, you are committing a crime.

But it is possible to get off of freeways. Not always easy, but possible. And whenever you take the trouble to do so, you pull away the state Highway Department's multimillion dollar mask, and get a glimpse of the real face of whatever place you happen to be.

We stopped one afternoon and had lunch in the shade of an old Catholic church in the town of Madison—population, probably a few hundred. It's a quiet little place up in the grain belt country above Sacramento. Dogs sleep in the streets. The fire department is voluntary. The sewing circle meets on Thursdays. And roosters wake the people up each morning.

When you spend most of your days in a metropolis, it's nice to know you still have such places as Madison to escape to for a quiet lunch. It's like having a bank account.

Up near the edge of the rolling wine country of Napa, there is a 17-mile stretch called the Calistoga Road. It's a winding ride, wrapping around tree-covered and stream-laced hills. The trees bend over the road from each side, and you can drive long distances without being able to see the sky.

It's a shame to live and die in California without ever taking this ride.

This country where we are camped, lashed by wind and rain one day and graced by sun the next, smells of the sea and its bounty. Huge vats of boiling red crabs, trays of fresh clams and perch filets, baskets of today's abalone. We have been eating well.

Our home in San Diego lies about as far south as Charleston, S.C.

Crescent City, further north on this coast, is almost as far north as Plymouth, Mass., and the cultures, from one tip to the other in this state, are about as far apart as their eastern counterparts.

But it's all California. It holds some of the hottest, coldest, wettest, and driest places of the Union. Some of the most fertile land. Some of the most barren.

No wonder people moved West.

The Duck Egg and I

Home is the wandering word chopper, home from high green hills. A few days in the sun turned me several shades darker, several dollars lighter.

Back to a neat stack of unopened bills. Back to work. Back to the income tax deadline.

(Back to the wall. Help!)

Actually, I had my income tax done for me while I was on vacation. Laid in the sun and let somebody else subtract line C from line D.

We drove back into town on Easter Saturday. A few blocks away from home, we suddenly remembered—our last house burned down last Easter Saturday.

We had been away to the beach, same as this year.

My wife said: "I'm going to keep my eyes closed. You just tell me if it's still there."

It *was* kind of a creepy feeling, driving down the last block.

However, last year's cloud produced this year's silver lining.

Boy, you should *see* the deductions you can get on income tax when your house burns down!

Speaking of deductions, we brought home another dependent. Not actually a deductible, but another mouth to feed.

This is a baby mallard duck named Mort. Property and responsibility of one 17-year-old son.

I was against the idea until I was informed that Mort's mother was a chicken. Stepmother, actually. Mort's egg was found and placed under a nesting hen just to see what happened. Mort happened.

("My, my," clucked his mother, "how am I ever going to explain *you*?")

I let the boy have the duck. Figured I could always get some verbal mileage out of a duck with a chicken for a mother.

Mort sits in his cage and peeps. I suppose that's the way his mother taught him to talk. We'll probably have to teach him to quack.

Back to spring in San Diego. On the road in Northern California, we ran into a different kind of weather four or five times a day.

We drove through the just budding vineyards of the Napa Valley and the San Joaquin.

There's a wine tasting room every few miles on these roads. "Stop and taste our wines." There's no charge.

You could stay smashed in that country for days and never spend a dime. (I often noticed Highway Patrol cars cruising near winery rooms. Probably pretty good territory.)

"Now we've got to pitch in and really clean up the house," said the wife. "From top to bottom."

Why is this? This is because some of the people we visited last week are going to visit us next week. (We play the vacation bit a little like musical chairs.)

She said: "We've got to do the carpets, the windows, and the walls. I don't know *where* to start."

I said: "Where's all that wine we bought up there? I think I'll just taste a little glass."

Then I went out in the garage, sat down and had a little chat with Mort. I taught him a few words in duck.

A Rainy Day Session

A morning of hard, driving rain. The paper said "a chance of light showers." I took a chance and walked to work. I nearly drowned.

Do schools still have rainy day sessions? When I was slapping erasers together, we had such a thing.

A few sprinkles and the school would switch over into it. Red lights would glow. Classes would be shortened. Lunch hour would be cut in half.

And we would get out of school about two hours early.

I don't have the slightest idea *why* it was bad for us to be in school when it was raining. But I can recall being all for it at the time.

The teachers seemed to like it too. (I expect it was their idea in the first place.)

Every Sunday during the dry season, Father Donohue would end mass with a request that we all "pray for rain."

We school children all prayed like crazy.

"Dear God, please let it rain—sometime during the week."

I was in real rain country last week. Far up the northern coast of California. (A weather story in Crescent City is when it doesn't rain.)

Saw a lot of signs: "Night crawlers for sale."

A night crawler is just that. A big red worm that crawls around on lawns at night, after a rain. They are used for fish bait.

The difference (to a trout) between a night crawler and a regular old worm is like the difference between a rib roast and a hamburger.

A place where they sell different kinds of worms is called a "worm ranch." It's a California term.

Will Rogers made note of that. He said he was never so hot as a cowboy, so he was thinking of moving to California and buying a worm ranch.

He said the ranch consisted of "two-thousand yearling worms, two-thousand 2-year-olds, five-hundred bull worms, and the rest a mixed herd."

I decided to have a little rainy day session for myself, and went home early. The younger children were all outside playing in the puddles. (On nice, sunny days they stay inside and watch TV.)

I got out the last logs of winter and started a blazing fire in the fireplace.

The new kittens were ambushing each other from room to room.

I settled down in the big leather chair with a glass of sherry and a thin volume of Southwell's poetry.

"May never was the month of love,
"For May is full of flowers:
"But rather April, wet by kind,
"For love is full of showers."

The wife came in from the kitchen and joined me. I said: "So what's the day's news? Who's in love? Who's out? Who's switched their careers? Who's on a diet? Who's in the middle of a crisis?"

She said: "Listen, you wouldn't believe this day."

(And there, journalism students, is where you get new ideas, day after day.)

Preferably Small Boys

In recent years, since moving down from the mountains, much of my free time is spent beside the sea, preferably in the company of small boys.

Almost any kind of small boy will do. A son, a nephew, a neighbor's son—all of them are pretty much the same.

If I happen to be out of small boys at that particular time that I am ready to head for the ocean's edge, I will take a small girl. But girls are second best, in this particular category. They lack the curiosity of the boy about the residents of tidepools, are afraid to touch a good many things, and usually are ready to go home before I am.

Not so with boys. They cannot sit still and play in the sand. The blood of explorers is in them, and they must be constantly

moving, picking up, studying something else that moves, and asking questions. They are perfectly willing to stay on the beach forever, as long as we bring along something to eat.

The small boys and I learn much from the sea, and from each other.

We study the fiddler crab, the curious little creature the Japanese call "siho maneki," which translates as "beckoning for the return of the tide." The tiny crab, indeed, seems to be doing just that, as he motions a "come here" sign with his one large claw.

But we know that the fiddler crab actually digs its burrow as far as it can get from the tide without actually abandoning the seas.

I learned this from a small boy, who read it to me from a book. Then we went down to the sea to check it out, and found that it was absolutely true.

Other crabs interest us. The little hermit crab, the clown of the tidepools, is worth watching for hours.

They spend practically every moment eating, looking for a mate and fighting among themselves. It appears none of them ever hurts each other.

Their only real problem is house hunting. The little, soft-bodied creature lives in borrowed or stolen shells, and must constantly change homes. At times, it does this to accommodate its growing body. But usually it is merely done on some compulsive whim.

Once the boys and I put some hermit crabs in an aquarium with some extra shells. It was like watching a game of musical chairs.

A small girl will seldom accompany you out on the mud flats. They deem it "ucky." But mud is one of a small boy's natural elements, and he will jump at the chance to get on a mud flat. (And to have a good deal of the mud flat get on him.)

There we find a variety of clams and many curious types of sea worms. (Seldom of the least bit of interest to girls.)

Some years ago, a couple of small boys and I tried to dig up a geoduck (pronounced "gooey-duck") clam on the mudflats of Tomales Bay, about 40 miles above San Francisco.

We spotted the clam's long siphon on one turn of the shovel, and it retracted deeper into the sand. We kept digging and so, seemingly, did the clam. Finally, about four feet down, we gave up. We could not keep the mud from collapsing in our hole, and we could not catch the clam.

I said: "I think that clam has as much energy as we do, boys. And he could probably stay a shovelful ahead of us all the way to China."

So we washed ourselves off as well as we could, then drove down the road a mile to a small cafe where we ordered a couple dozen raw oysters, one beer and two oranges.

Raw oyster lunches are another thing small girls aren't much good for.

Don't Lie to My Body

A lot of gloomy days lately. Summer can't seem to get started. A friend sent me a postcard from blue Hawaii. Palm trees. Golden sun. A wahine in a bikini. (Thanks friend!)

The children are checking off the days till summer. "It's *never* coming," they moaned.

Gloomy weather is not so bad when you are still in school. It's the bright, sunny days that are killing. You sit in the classroom all through May with eyes glued on the windows.

Now they pop Daylight Savings time on us. It doesn't help in the morning.

The clock says it is 6 o'clock, but my body knows that is a lie. My body knows it is 5 o'clock. Who can function at such an hour?

I said: "All right, you guys, I know you're awake. Roll out of that sack—*now!*"

A cold morning. And everybody's battery is run down.

On rainy days, an occasional lizard moves into the house with us. (This bugs me a little, but delights the small boys.)

The other morning, after a small storm, the children were creeping into their school clothes.

The oldest girl was getting into her blue jeans. However, a rained out lizard had already taken up residence in one of the legs.

She got the jeans all the way on before she felt the lizard. And then—"*aaaggghhhh!*"

I mean, I have *never* seen a household come to life so fast!

There was one sunny day last week—on my day off. (A silver lining if there ever was one.)

I let the youngest moppet ditch nursery school. We took off all by ourselves and spent the day at Sea World. It was very educational, and she decided on her future career during the day.

Somehow, we had never taken her to the Japanese pearl diving show. The girl divers and the lovely ladies in kimonos who served us tea completely fascinated her.

At the end of the afternoon, she announced: "Now I know what I'm going to be when I grow up."

I said: "Well, thank goodness one of you has decided. What are you going to be?"

She said: "A Japanese lady."

The Night of Agnes Larkin

So we come to the end of April, a misty month of fog and showers. May comes in on a full moon.

It is Walpurgis night in Europe tonight. The Witches' Sabbath. (I whispered this slowly to a daughter, then said: "Boo!" She jumped a foot.)

Tomorrow also begins American Camping Week. However, we beat the rush. We had our American Camping Week earlier this month.

My wife, two daughters and I stayed in a small camper on the wind and rain lashed coast up in Northern California.

At night, while the ocean pounded and the rain hammered the

camper, the four of us sat inside and told ghost stories by the flickering light of one candle.

(The truth is, only two of us sat. The two girls huddled in their bunk and listened to the stories with the covers over their heads.)

It was delicious. We scared ourselves silly.

We did not tell conventional ghost stories. We made them up—a few sentences at a time.

One person would start a story, get the characters into some creepy situation, then tell the person to the left: "Okay, you take over."

We competed with each other to make the story scarier and scarier.

"Once upon a time there was a strange old lady named Agnes Larkin, who lived in a humble little cottage by the sea. She had been extremely weird since she was a girl of seven, when—Okay, you take over."

". . . her hair turned a dull white . . ."

(Sounds of "Ooooooh" and "Oh Boy!" from the listeners.)

". . . anyway her hair had turned dull white because one day, as she was walking along the beach, she saw a figure approach her on the sand. The figure was singing a strange song in German. It was limping, and carrying a glass of blood and—Okay, you take over."

". . . and . . . and, it was a baby, only two months old!"

("Ooooohhh! Oh Boy!" Heads dived under the covers!)

Anyway, you get the idea. As we progressed, the story got absolutely terrifying. Bodies here and there throughout a castle. Agnes Larkin's ghost roaming around. That baby walking around, singing strange German songs. The wind making the camper creak.

". . . and standing behind the baby that night, his arms raised high, stood a seven foot giant with a huge, shining ax in his hands. . . ."

My wife said: "Okay, I think that's about enough for tonight. I think we should get some sleep now!"

". . . and, suddenly, the ax swung downward . . ."

"I *said* I think we ought to get some *sleep* now!"

It *was* getting pretty frightening, so we stopped.

We blew out the candle, pulled up the covers, closed our eyes and listened to the storm.

And *nobody* slept—for a long, long time.

The School Open House

We marched off to the nearest grammar school the other evening for the annual open house for parents. Coffee, cookies, a view of the children's classwork and a quick rap session with the teacher. (Later the kid gets rapped. "Do you know your teacher said you *could* be getting straight A's if you would just *apply* yourself?)

I must have heard that, myself, a thousand times when I was slapping erasers.

(Who wanted to get straight A's, except maybe some girl? Who wanted to be a social outcast?)

I go to open house now to look at the compositions. A lot of it is pretty good stuff. (And I admit it—I take notes sometimes. It's a tough business, and you get your material where you can.)

I think I like the third grade compositions best. They are loaded with imagination.

For instance:

"I had a dream that I was in New York and there was a mummy on the lose and I helped all the police in getting the people out of the town. But we could not capture the mummy and it kept following me. Even when I left the city on a boat the mummy was following in a boat, and I woke up and then I asked my mother can a mummy row a boat?"

Wow! A mummy in a rowboat! How can you put material like that down?

Dinosaurs were big in the art show this year. We must have seen a dozen pictures of dinosaurs on the walls. Big dinosaurs. Small ones. There was one dinosaur with a cowboy riding on back.

(Did you know the dinosaur became extinct from back damage? Bending over, picking weeds and grass. Let that be a lesson to you, man.)

A lot of pictures of cowboys and airplanes. Flowers and children playing ring-around-the-rosy.

After the art show and coffee, I went back to the third grade and read more compositions.

"Six cowboys were sitting around a campfire when a bunch of Indians came up. The cowboys were scared but they were friendly Indians and did not fire. So everybody sat down and had some coffee and the Indians told the cowboys where the hunting was good and the cowboys gave the Indians some food and some tobasco to smoke and the Indians rode away."

I'll bet that kid could write a sequel to that story.

About what happened when the Indians came back—after smoking that tobasco.

How to Play the Heartstrings

"Dad, do you have any extra jobs I can do around here to earn some extra money?"

There's one of the household early birds, scratching around for a worm.

I said: "What do you need money for?"

He said: "I want to buy a new pair of pants."

I said: "Look, I don't even know what you mean by the term 'extra money.' However, it is my understanding that the law requires me to keep you in pants. So forget about the 'extra jobs.' Just do your regular jobs, and I may give you some plain old, regular money for pants."

From another quarter comes: "Can I have a dollar besides my bus fare?"

I said: "No! What do you want a dollar for?"

"I just wanted to buy mom a Mother's Day present."

"Oh—well, all right, here."

(Now that's the way to bag a worm, birdies. Lure him out with a tender tune on the heartstrings.)

From money to Mother's Day without ever changing the subject. "What are you going to get mom?"

I said: "I don't know. I've been thinking of a lighted make-up mirror for the bedroom."

She said: "Why would I need that?"

I said: "You *weren't* supposed to hear that. But, as long as you did, a makeup mirror in the bedroom might allow a little more traffic in the main bathroom each morning."

(A daughter whispered: "I thought she wanted a Yoga outfit." I whispered back: "I can't even buy her a scarf the right size.")

The honoree said: "It isn't necessary to get me anything special."

I said: "How about breakfast in bed Sunday morning?"

She said: "Could you make it lunch?"

Mother's Day was invented by Anna Jarvis (Miss Anna Jarvis) of Philadelphia in 1907—(long after mothers were invented.)

President Wilson made it official in 1914. (President Wilson was reelected in 1916.)

Lively days around the nursery school these days. Mother's Day is a theme they can get their teeth into.

We pick up the youngest moppet about 4 p.m. She says: "We're making something for you for Mother's Day but I can't tell you."

Then she says: "I'll whisper it to you, cause it's a secret."

(You can't *tell* your mother what you're making, because it's a secret. If you only whisper it to her, that's different. It stays in the secret class.)

Happy Mother's Day.

Mother was blessed with cards and presents and breakfast in bed over the weekend. Father turned into some kind of a creepy monster. It was the weekend he gave the kittens away.

People kept walking around giving me looks usually reserved for child beaters and old lady muggers.

I said: "For Pete's sake, we couldn't keep them forever. I already let you stall a couple of weeks."

She said: "They were *very* little."

I said: "Look, we promised those two girls kittens. What do you want to do, wait and give them a couple of old cats?"

The news went out over the telephone. "Yes, they went today. They looked *so* helpless and pitiful. I went back to my room and *cried*."

All our bad news gets on the telephone immediately. If something bad is happening, spread it, man, spread it.

There's a lot of talk about phones being tapped by the government these days. I'll bet if ours is tapped, somebody in the government cried himself to sleep last night.

(I'll probably get a card in the government files. That's what they do with monsters.)

The sun came out for awhile. Spring danced on our hillsides. I said: "Hey, how about going to the beach, or maybe cooking some hamburgers in the park?"

A child said: "How would you like it if somebody gave you away when you were only a few weeks old?"

I said: "How would *you* like it if somebody gave *you* away when you were only a teen-ager? Now cut it out!"

The wife came home from the grocery store, and started unloading groceries. "Oh goodness, I got too much cat food. I . . . forgot."

I said: "Will you *please* close that subject! How could you get too much cat food, anyway? It comes in *cans*! It'll last forever."

She said: "You don't have to yell. I merely meant I got more than we really need . . . anymore."

(She merely meant that heartless people should be reminded of it over and over.)

The kittens went to two perfectly good homes. They are the only cats in their new households.

They are probably spoiled rotten already. Dining on steak and cream, and a whole new set of drapes to tear up.

I said: "I'm famished. What's for dinner?"

She said: "I'm not sure yet. I haven't really figured it out."

A moping child said: "I'm not hungry. I don't think I could eat tonight."

I said: "Well, I think I could eat tonight. I'm starved."

So I fixed myself a sandwich and a beer and sat down and ate. Alone. (Nobody would sit down at the same table with Jack the Ripper.)

I said: "Look, would it get me out of trouble if I promised to take you kids to visit the kittens sometime?"

They said: "Oh, wow! That'd be neat. Could we go tomorrow?"

Peace, my children.

Summer is a Bikini

Trembling on the brink of summer here. We tested one of our beaches the other afternoon. Mama mia! That'sa some cold'a water!

"Aren't you going to take a bathing suit, or at least cutoffs?" I asked the seventh-grader. "Just in case you want to go in the water."

"Nah," he said. "It's still way too cold."

However, an hour later he was swimming around all over the bay. And swimming fully clothed, to boot.

How this came to be is an eternal story.

We were sitting on the blanket after donating a blue and a red kite to wherever it is that runaway kites and unbroken soap bubbles go. Suddenly, romance came walking down the beach wearing a couple of junior miss size bikinis.

"Hi. Would you hold our dog while we go for a swim?"

"Huh . . oh . . yeah . . sure."

Ten minutes later, the dog was tied to a lamppost, and our

water-shy lad was swimming, in his jeans and shirt, with the two girls out to an island.

His mother said: "That's insanity."

I said: "Nope. It's incentive."

However, the episode ended tragically. Thirty minutes later he was back, dripping wet, shivering, and disillusioned.

He said: "Heck, they're only sixth graders."

Romance is mathematically balanced according to ages in those tender years. To a seventh grader, a sixth grader is a mere chid. An eighth grade girl is an old woman!

I remember meeting a girl at one of those get-acquainted dances in high school. After spending the entire dance together, I found out she was a senior and she found out I was a freshman.

We were both horrified.

(Later I bragged about it. But I'll bet she never said a single word on the subject.)

He said: "They sure didn't look like sixth graders."

I said: "Well, it's hard to tell when they're in a bikini."

The best of summer is yet to come. Iced tea, cold beer, baseball and balmy evenings.

There will be many more days at the beach. Many more summer girls in bikinis. (They should wear labels if they're only sixth graders, but where would they wear them?)

Some of us go to the beach for *other* reasons. We go for the suntan—the brown badge of summer. It's a status thing. ("What do you want to do, look like a tourist?")

Some of us do not turn golden brown. Some of us turn a hot red.

I am one of those. By Friday evening, you can peel the previous Sunday afternoon right off my back.

The wife—hah! She is one of the golden brown ones except—except, that her nose turns bright red. The rest of her looks like a color photo in a travel magazine, but her nose always comes out like Rudolph the reindeer's.

And on Monday mornings she moans because she can't wear her orange pants suit to work "because it clashes with my nose."

The Longest Days

"There is no more wretched picture than a fair landscape framed by a school window." I wrote that one day during a poetry attack.

(These attacks don't last long. I can usually be pulled out of them by putting up the screens or going to the store for milk.)

However, school does seem to be becoming more unbearable every moment around here. It seems to take about six months to get through the last few weeks.

A phone call came from the school nurse. "He's just feeling dizzy, but I don't think he should try to make it home by himself."

I hopped into the family ambulance and headed for Roosevelt Junior High.

The dizzy kid was stretched out on a cot in the nurse's office. He didn't *look* faint or pale. He looked rosy as a rose.

(Earlier in the day, he had been a nervous wreck because he couldn't find his gym clothes. "I'll get another non-suit," he moaned.)

I said: "From the evidence in this case, I deduce that the precise moment you became faint and dizzy was just before your physical education period. Right?"

Right.

The Sherlock Holmes of the suburbs.

I brought him home and he flaked out on the couch. I said: "Do you still feel dizzy?" He said: "Yeah, kinda."

I said: "Maybe it would clear up a little if you turned off the television."

Thirty minutes later, another offspring came pedaling up the sidewalk.

"I felt so tired, I couldn't stay at school a minute longer."

I said: "You were so pooped you got on your bike and rode right home—four miles?"

She said: "I'm going to go lie down in my room."

Sometimes I write at home. Mostly during the school year when people are *in* school. It's peaceful. The coffee's handy. And the cats make good paperweights.

However, when the house fills up with children, all systems

are switched on. The television. The stereo. (In fact, *two* stereos!) The piano.

This blows a fuse in my system. And the typing paper sits there in the typewriter, giving me this blank stare.

Another child came strolling through the front door. "I skipped the last two periods. There's really nothing for me to do in them."

The wife called from work. I said: "Just about *every*body's home already!"

She said: "What are you going to do?"

I said: "I feel tired and dizzy. I think I'll go to the office."

Golden sun and sky blue skies. We are easing into summer around here as painlessly as possible.

"Could you build us a tree house?" the moppets implored.

I said: "Are you kidding? A tree house built by an adult is worthless. Only a small boy can build a tree house that's any good."

"What about girls?" said the girl.

I said: "Girls can help. They're good for holding nails and handing up the saw. But fathers are absolutely no good at all on tree houses."

Building a tree house is a temporary gift that goes away at about the age of 12 or 13.

I do have one building project for myself. I intend to install a hammock in the backyard. Then I intend to install myself in the hammock.

Wake me when it's September.

A Little Something Missing

"Oh, the summer night has a smile of light,
"And she sits on a sapphire throne."

Somewhere there are summer nights like that. Stars so thick in the sky it's hard to pick some of them apart. A warm stillness and fireflies dancing under the trees.

But not in San Diego.

That's no rap on our weather. Who else has it so good? You can live here without an air conditioner, and, if you have to, without heat. An overcoat shop would fold here in a week.

We have no blizzards, no hurricanes, no cyclones, no big freezes, no huge snowstorms, no really long rains, no slush in the streets, no sandstorms, no searing heat waves.

But we also have no fireflies.

I wish the zoo would look into this. Maybe trade an extra sloth or so to some poor little zoo in Iowa for a couple of hundred fireflies.

They would certainly brighten up the summer nights.

I first collected fireflies in the Ozarks, along the banks of a river whose name I never knew. (I was 10, and we had gone there by train from Oregon to return my grandmother's body to the lonely hills where she was born.)

We collected the glowing little bugs in the glass Mason jars and carried them around like lanterns.

(I also rode a pig bareback and traded eggs for candy at a little general store when I was back there. I'll never forget that trip.)

I next saw fireflies while sitting on a friend's front porch in Cedar Rapids.

We sat there sipping iced tea and watching the kids turn the crank of a wooden ice cream freezer. And the fireflies blinked off and on under the maple trees.

A midsummer evening in middle America.

Fireflies are really beetles. They light up—at the beginning of an upward or downward course—because of a unique chemical reaction.

They also use their lighting system to find their mates. ("Hey, Edna, is that you over there? Shine your light over here.")

In tropical jungles, men sometimes attach fireflies to their boots to light the path in front of them.

And in Cuba, women sometimes pin fireflies on their gowns, or attach them to a golden chain.

Don't know whether fireflies just wouldn't like the California climate, or whether they are barred along with the other bugs at the state border.

But I imagine they could be a big success in the Golden State. (I suspect the hippies would really dig them. "Psychedelic, man!")

Anyway, it's all wishful thinking. There are no fireflies in California, and won't be. (And kids can't ride pigs bareback or trade eggs for candy at a general store.)

I guess we'll have to settle for neon.

Father is the Delicate One

Summer is one day old today. It began at exactly 5:20 yesterday afternoon. (I celebrated it a little.)

Father's Day turned out splendid. I got a new hammock, all set up under the pepper tree in the back yard.

"You scared us to death when you wrote you were going to put up a hammock," said the wife. "The kids and I already had it picked out and ordered."

I said: "Is that right?"

(I had mentioned it only slightly before. I thought one more hint wouldn't hurt.)

Also got a splendid weekend for two at a resort hotel. Splendid swimming pool. (Splendid sunburn!)

We came home and she said: "Now then, why don't you just go lie down on your hammock?"

I said: "I don't think I can lie down on anything. I feel as if I'd been boiled."

Anyway, nothing was too good for father over the weekend. I've got the receipts to prove it.

Life changes for everybody in the summer. The children are all home from school. (That's when I start writing at the office again.)

The nursery school chick came up to me in the back yard the other afternoon and said: "There's nothing to do."

I said: "My goodness, only five years old and you've done everything worth doing."

She said: "Well, there *isn't*."

I said: "Why don't you go pick up your room."

She said: "I mean there's nothing to do that's *fun*. That's no fun."

Tragic when you're five years old and all the fun has gone out of life.

She said: "I could paint if you could go get me some water paints at the store."

I said: "Anything to save an empty life." (The clay pigeon of Seaside Surburbia—shot down again.)

I put a little lotion on and took some of the fire out of the sunburn. (It took me about a half hour to put it on. Touchy business.)

She said: "I don't know why you turn so red. I was out there as long as you were."

I said: "It's simply a matter of whether you have delicate skin or whether you are made of leather. I am sort of like the princess who couldn't sleep with a pea under her mattress."

(Some people just turn brown as Apaches. Some people could sleep with a crate of peas under their mattress.)

Opened a beer and went out to test the new hammock. There was a cat on it. Sound asleep.

I said: "Rover, get the — get off my hammock."

He opened one eye, looked up at me, then closed it again.

Oh well. Rover's a father, too. (We think.)

A Duel in the Desert

"On a dark midnight, far out on the Nevada desert, two men with guns in their hands stood back to back, waiting for a signal from a third man.

"One of the armed men was me."

I *love* to tell this story to my children, nephews, and nieces. It is absolutely true, and sometimes I build it up so much, I scare myself.

I start the story in the middle, and add dramatic touches: ". . . as the third man gave the signal, a moanful cry of something hurt swept through the desert night."

By this time, the hairs on the back of the kids' necks are usually standing at attention.

". . . and both of us slowly clicked back the hammers on our weapons. Mine was a .38 caliber Smith & Wesson Police Special; his, a .30-30 Winchester carbine, with which I had seen him hit a can tossed in the air twice before it touched the ground."

The bug-eyed kids are now demanding: "Did you win? Did you win?"

I say: "Hold on, podners. I'm here, ain't I?"

As I said, the story is true. But it is not exactly what it sounds like. Still, there was plenty of drama involved.

Two friends and I were returning from a deer hunting trip in Utah several years ago. It was a trip we had taken together several times, and our habit was to drive straight through in both directions.

It was a long haul, from our hunting grounds to home, and it usually took about 24 hours, including meal stops—and a little handle pulling in Nevada.

But the desert is a long, monotonous run—especially at night. Sometimes you can drive for an hour without seeing another set of headlights.

One night—that dark midnight—we were bored and aching from the ride, when one of my friends said: "Hey, let's try some of my animal calls. Maybe we can roust up a coyote."

Well, the procedure was this. Two of us stood back to back, guns in our hands and flashlights held straight up (so as not to be seen, but to catch the glint in the eyes of any approaching animal), while the third man crouched near us and blew the animal call.

The call simulated the cries of a wounded rabbit in distress.

It was quiet on the desert floor, and I seem to recall a faint moon. We walked about 100 yards off the silent highway and got into position.

Poised and ready, we stood there for several minutes while the counterfeit cries of animal pain poured through the night.

Suddenly, we spotted a light. A headlight. A car came up the highway from a distance, slowed as it neared our parked car, then stopped.

Its occupants must have spotted that eerie scene of two armed men, back to back, in the night. For, suddenly, the car sped away, screeching and leaving tire rubber on the dark highway.

No animals came, but the night left memories for us.

I wonder what kind of memories it left for whomever was in that car?

The Semi-Barefoot Boy

It will be a considerable boon to mankind's economic and emotional security when it becomes fashionable to wear mismatched socks.

Confucius did not say that. I said that. But, it is no less profound.

How can a man open his sock drawer and find 30 socks, and every blooming one of them a different color? It is a question I have only been asking since I began wearing socks.

What would be wrong with wearing mismatched socks? Say purple on one foot, green on the other. It would be an interesting dash of color.

I was raised in a gray, conservative age when everything had to match. The most horrible thing anybody could think of was wearing something blue with something green.

Now, the fashions are wild and colorful. Everything goes with everything else.

Still, from our ankles down, we are bound in 19th century tradition. And, on a morning when we cannot find matching socks, the hosiery industry and the people who make tranquilizers continue to get rich.

With my back against the wall, I said: "I think I'll wear one gray sock and one orange sock today."

My clothes critic said: "Don't be silly. There must be some matching socks downstairs in the laundry."

I said: "What's silly? Guys I know wear red slacks and purple ties and orange leather jackets. What's wrong with mixing up the socks once in awhile."

She said: "You fix the coffee. I'll go look for some socks."

What I think I will do is throw out all these single socks and go downtown and buy about 30 pairs of socks all the same color. Some kind of color that will go with anything. Maybe a nice warm khaki.

She came upstairs and said: "Here. I found a pair of orange ones."

I said: "With blue slacks and a green shirt?"

She said: "At least they match."

The problem is, if I buy socks all the same color, I would have to pick a color or a pattern that my sons would not wear. (And can you think of anything a teenager would not wear today?)

Once I bought some pink socks. The boys thought they were pretty kinky. Then, one day, they decided it would be a good idea to dress kinky. They bagged my pink socks.

Later, they returned them. And I still have one.

Then I bought some longer socks. The high, calf hugger types. I figured my boys would never wear this kind of "old man's sock."

They wouldn't. But the girls said: "Oh, neat! Knee socks!" (I still have *one* of those, too.)

I see only two possible solutions. One is to become a cowboy and wear cowboy boots. I know some cowboys, and I know they do not always wear matched socks.

Some cowboys I know do not even wear socks.

The only other answer, I guess, is men's panty hose.

A Dark and Stormy Night

The rain came slashing down, and the midnight wind whipped around the house. I could hear the trees outside creaking, and the power lines moaning.

And it seemed as if I heard a door open downstairs.

I thought to myself: No, that can't be a burglar. Why would a burglars work on a night like this?

And I lay there with my eyes wide open, listening.

I heard footsteps, and a kind of a thumping.

Silly, I thought, that thumping is just your heart. Yeah, but what about the *footsteps*? Those weren't mine. I was flat on my back.

I thought: If there *is* a burglar down there, maybe he would be scared away if I made some kind of noise.

So I pushed a heavy book off my nightstand.

"What was that?" said the wife, sitting up in bed.

I said: "Shhh. It's nothing I just knocked a book off the nightstand."

She said: "Why are you whispering?"

I said: "I think there may be a burglar in the house. Ow! You're digging your nails in my arm."

The footsteps stopped. Then I heard some dishes rattling.

"What's that?" she said.

I said: "Dishes. Maybe he's hungry. Maybe he'll just eat and go away."

She said: "Aren't you going to do something? Aren't you going down there?"

I said: "I'm not hungry. Let him eat by himself. Besides, he may have a gun."

She said: "Don't we have a gun? Where is it?

I said: "It's all over the place. I took it apart and scattered the pieces in different places so the kids couldn't fire it. It would take me three days to find it all."

She said: "Well, what *are* we going to do?"

I said: "How do you feel about screaming?"

I felt around for some kind of weapon. I couldn't see a blinking thing in the dark and I didn't think it would be a good idea to turn on the light.

Finally, my hand touched my portable typewriter. It was heavy, at least, and better than nothing. (Besides, I thought, if anything happened to me, it would be sort of like a cowboy cashing in with his boots on.)

"Be careful," she hissed. "He may be really dangerous."

I said: "Maybe I ought to go back to bed and wait a while longer."

She said: "He may come up here if you do."

So, I crept downstairs very slowly. In fact, it took me about 10 minutes. And I slipped through the living room and peeked cautiously into the kitchen.

There, at the table, was a son, eating a mountain of ice cream.

I said: "What are you doing up at this time of night?"

He said: "The rain woke me up and then I felt hungry. What are you doing with the typewriter, dad?"

I said: "Oh . . . uh . . . it was kind of in the way upstairs, so I thought I'd bring it down here. Goodnight."

He said: "You're weird, dad."

The Animal Parade

The sun finally came out and blessed all our beasts and children. With a sunny smile on his face, the 11-year-old boy took his pet armadillo to school.

That would be Thorndyke. (The armadillo. Not the boy.)

"They asked me to bring him for display," he said. "So when

people come to look at him, I'll stand around and say, 'Hi. That's my armadillo—Thorndyke.' "

I imagine having your own armadillo is a pretty big status thing in the fifth grade. (The closest thing I ever came to one at that age was a horny toad.)

Thorndyke, by and large, makes an excellent pet. He's very interesting to look at, what with being built like a small tank. Armadillo means "little armored thing."

He is no behavior problem around the house, and no cost at all to feed.

Thorndyke is stuffed.

His spirit has gone to that great armadillo burrow in the sky, but his body can be seen in a display case at Grant School on open house night next week.

A lot of unusual pets have passed through my life. (A lot of them have gone to their rewards, too. Good thing we didn't have them all stuffed. We wouldn't have room to walk around here.)

There were Bonny and Clyde, the hamsters. A variety of frogs and toads from the time I had pockets in my pants through the time my sons did.

There was Curley, the clumsy cat. So awkward, he fell down the stairs at least once a day.

There was another cat, whose name I forget, that accidentally went to eternity in a spin dryer. (Maybe her name was Fluffy. She certainly ended up *looking* fluffy.)

There was Mort, the mallard duck, who practiced flying in the backyard until he finally got the hang of it. Then he headed for Acapulco. A self-made duck.

I once bought my children half of a donkey. (I know, I know. Which half?)

This donkey was bought by another reporter and me for $12.50 each from a bartender friend. He said some guy had given him the animal when he couldn't pay his bar bill.

Anyway, we boarded Lightning Charlie at a friend's ranch on the edge of town. And every other weekend we would take the kids out to the ranch and let them ride him.

Now, the only trouble is, a donkey that is ridden only every other week does not take kindly to being ridden at all.

Lightning Charlie would sit there and refuse to move his front legs. However, he was perfectly willing to move his back legs anytime somebody got near them. He moved them in a kicking direction.

And, if he could not reach you with his hind legs, he would attempt to take a hunk out of you with his teeth.

We finally just quit showing up at the ranch, and Charlie died a couple of years later. "Don't know what from," our friend said, "but I'd guess it was from pure meanness."

That animal probably would have been a lot more cooperative if we'd had him stuffed from the very beginning.

Home Can Be Hazardous to Your Health

As everyone in this household knows, the handiest place to leave something such as a coat, a toy, a coffee cup, or homework is on the stairs.

I slipped on something the other day and took the last three steps sitting down.

"Damn!" I just happened to mention.

"What happened?"

"What does it look like happened? I was in a hurry to get downstairs so I decided it would be faster to fall down them."

As safety people have pointed out time and time again, eight out of 10 accidents happen in the household.

Home is where you grab the wrong bottle of pills in the night.

Home is where you hit your head on a shelf.

Home is where you hammer your thumb to a board.

I said: "When are people going to stop leaving things on the stairs?"

Home is where you hang your hat. And yourself.

Misty days around here. The children all stacked up in the house after school. They put a record on the stereo.

When they got the volume up loud enough—to a point where the drinking glasses were trembling in the cupboard—they went into another room and watched TV.

They left the TV and came into the kitchen. One daughter said: "Can we cook up a batch of spaghetti? We learned how in school."

I said: "Sure, live it up. I'm glad you're learning to cook, since it doesn't look like you're going to make it as a movie starlet."

She said: "The best way to tell if the spaghetti is cooked just right is to toss a piece of it up, and if it sticks to the ceiling it's done."

I said: "*Good Grief*! Is that what they taught you in cooking?"

It doesn't look promising. I doubt if there are many young men out looking for a bride who flings spaghetti at the ceiling.

"Where the devil is the hammer?" I shouted. "I remember putting it right here in this drawer."

"What do you want the hammer for?"

I said: "What *would* I want a hammer for? I want it so I can beat myself on the head because everything in this house ends up on the stairs except the spaghetti. And that goes on the kitchen ceiling."

She said: "I think I saw it out in the yard, by the daisy bed. The kids must have left it out there."

(What are they doing? Beating my daisies to death?)

I found the hammer and went to work on a little home repair project. A kitchen drawer needed a few nails.

I had to use those little short nails. The kind that are not as long as your finger is wide.

I promptly hammered my fingers.

"*Ouch*!" I casually noted.

"What happened?"

"Nothing happened," I said. "I was just trying out my scream."

Some days.

Pretty Goot for an Old Finn

"A lady is here to see you," said the guard at the Second Avenue door. "I think you'd better come down here. I don't want to send her up there."

The old woman sat at the bottom of the stairs in this beat-up wheelchair, wearing a pair of ragged blue jeans and one of the trouser legs was empty. And all I could say, under my breath, was "Oh boy, one of those."

Five minutes before, there had been a promise of summer in the air, the golf game was only an hour away, and the last thing I needed was somebody else's troubles.

And this looked like professional hard-lucker No. 847.

The old woman seemed to sense this, and she appeared to be as uncomfortable in the situation as me. Maybe my phony smile tipped her off.

I probably should have had my face slapped.

Because, it turned out that Mayme Mattson was not "one of those."

In fact it turned out that Mayme Mattson is one of the really lucky people around. She's one of the happy ones.

Mayme has her troubles okay, probably more than most, but she also has the answer to them that always seems to elude so many. Mayme has what she herself would probably call, in her thick Finnish accent, a definite "tings-shure-could-be-vorse" kind of philosophy.

What Mayme wanted was a new wheelchair. Not a gift, necessarily, but a chance to earn one.

"Ay am a goot baby-sitter," she said, "und ay can make pretty goot dolls and poodles out of yarn."

She had come to the newspaper because she already had been everywhere else she could think of to go.

The old wheelchair really was a piece of junk. Mayme had wrapped the shredded rubber tires with friction tape, but it kept wearing through. Some spokes were broken, and it was getting harder, she said, to fold the rusty old thing up so she could crawl onto the city buses on her hands and knees.

That's why Mayme wears blue jeans, because she has to crawl when she's not in the wheelchair. A dress would be nicer to wear, but there are stairs in the little Navy housing project apartment where she lives with a daughter and six grandchildren, and crawling is the only way she can climb them.

Mayme's eyes were a blue-gray as pale as the worn spots on the knees of her jeans. But the eyes, unlike the jeans, still had their luster.

She said she was 62, three years away from a disability pension, but she giggled like a school-girl when she told little jokes on herself. Like about how she happens to be taking highschool French at the Midway Adult School.

It seems Mayme and her daughter, Jean, wife of a Navy storekeeper at sea, clipped coupons out of the Evening Tribune recently to get a Learn-A-Language record. They thought studying Spanish would give them something to fill the empty hours.

But they made a mistake marking the coupons and got French records instead of Spanish. So they studied French. Now both of them are signed up at Midway. Jean goes on Mondays and Mayme on Wednesdays.

"Und you know?" said Mayme, "yust today I answer three questions in class in French. Pretty goot for an old Finn, huh?"

Mayme isn't really a Finn. She's a native American, a miner's daughter born in Ironwood, Mich. But Finnish was what her parents spoke and she learned it before she learned English. So she has the accent.

She also was the wife of a miner until three years ago, when her husband died of a heart attack. He left her a $60 a month veteran's pension to live on, so a year later she moved to California to stay with the daughter. Michigan's miserable winters made life alone in a wheelchair more than difficult.

Mayme lost the lower half of her left leg 10 years ago, running for a bus. She stepped on a stone, fell to the ground, then limped around several days believing she had a sprain.

But it was a bad break and gangrene set in.

"Okay, so I lose my leg," she said. "But I do okay. I get around goot, und people help me get onto buses and things. I make a few dollars, too, with my dolls and poodles."

But right now, she had to face facts. The wheelchair was shot and so was the pension check. And without a wheelchair, there could be no French lessons. There would be no way to get out of the house at all.

Mayme didn't appear to like the idea at all, but she was asking for help.

Well, the chair was no particular problem. A phone call to the Salvation Army got her an almost new, tubular steel model!—a better one than she had ever had. The Salvation Amy shrugged it off with a that's-what-we're-around-for attitude. So Mayme got her chair.

We took it over to her in a taxi, and she crawled down the stairs and out on the front porch to meet us.

Her daughter had gone to the store and Mayme was babysitting. The grandkids, all under 11, crowded around to look at it and one little blonde beamed as she rubbed her hand along the clean metal spokes. "Oh, grandma, it's a pretty one," she said.

Mayme was happy and grateful and all that. And she asked me to thank the Salvation Army for her.

Then she added, "You know, I guess it's real tough on folks, not knowing what to do with people like us."

Deadly but Wonderful

The last real Fourth of July that I remember happened in Phoenix in 1939. That was in an innocent age before the world became safe and sane.

I can remember holding a long Roman candle in my hand and shooting multicolored fire bombs high into the evening.

We could—and did—buy firecrackers big enough to burst the seams of a tin can as it hurtled 30 feet high.

Cherry bombs were only slightly less powerful than hand grenades, and a good deal touchier.

Rockets were launched in a green Coke bottle, and made a blazing arc in the dusk. We hadn't the slightest idea where they landed.

Ladyfingers were the tiny little firecrackers, about half the size of a wooden match, which you let explode between your fingers to show the world, which consisted of the other kids in the neighborhood, that you were brave.

There was no question about it. Fireworks were dangerous. My father, who is an old man now, has lived most of his life with a thumb which he cannot bend, because he failed to fling one of those big firecrackers away in time.

Fireworks were deadly. But, somehow, they were absolutely wonderful.

You can still buy fireworks here and there. They aren't available in San Diego County, but you could drive up to San Clemente and find those little wooden, temporary stands that sell them.

But they are not the same as in 1939. For one thing, they are terribly expensive. A modest assortment of sparks and fizzles could cost you around $12.

And there is nothing in the items on sale that could even unnerve a cat. A few things that throw off a small pile of sparks. Some devices that whistle. But not a single thing that explodes.

This is all good and healthy I suppose. There are plenty of public fireworks displays. We can sit on a blanket and watch these in the evening without danger of injury.

Still, there is something in a boy, even if he is in his 40s, that wants to be the one to light the fuse.

The laws controlling fireworks have made us safer and saner. But they have taken something away from us.

A few July Fourths ago, I was in Mexico, where they still have marvelous fireworks. You can buy them all year around in some cities.

I was camped on the beach in San Felipe with my oldest son and one of his friends, and we had naturally bought a bundle of fireworks.

As darkness approached, that beach became a battleground. Firecrackers were exploding all around everybody.

Down at the water's edge, a couple of drunken campers were dueling at 50 paces with little penny rockets.

And, now and then, somebody would have to rush with a bucket of water to douse a burning spot on one of the tents.

I don't think anybody got hurt that evening. But I suppose they easily could have. It was decidedly dangerous.

And everybody had an absolute ball.

Bye, Bye Birdies

Bless the beasts and children. (If I didn't have them to write about, I would probably be back on the police beat.)

There's an awful mockingbird with a nest in one of our trees. He dive bombs the cats anytime they step out into the yard. A quick swoop down and a peck at their tail.

He is driving Deirdre and Rotten Ralph up the wall. Or, rather, under the house.

Also, he has a voice like George Burns. "Wawwk! Wawwk!"

A mockingbird, I read, is supposed to be able to imitate more than 32 other birds. But not this one. I think he picked up his sound from a Model A horn somewhere.

I went out in the yard and whistled up a few bird calls to give him some new material. I tried a "Bob White" and a quail call.

All I got back was "Wawwk! Wawwk!"

However, since he *is* a living creature that happens to live here, nothing would do but to give him a name. The children insisted.

So, we call him Frankenstein.

I once had a pet parakeet, or rather two pet parakeets. Neighbors swore I could teach them to talk if I was patient enough.

"Talk to them every day, using simple words."

I was patient enough. I talked to them every day. Simple little things like: "Hello birdie." And, "Talk, birdie." And, "Dammit, *talk* birdie!"

Nothing. Not a blooming word.

I fed them quality birdseed. In those days, the best birdseed came from marijuana plants. I thought maybe the birds were too stoned to talk.

Then, one day, I found a small egg in the nest.

Those birds weren't talking to me, but it seemed pretty clear they were on speaking terms with each other.

We rushed down to the pet store and told the lady who owned it the news.

Talk about over reaction. I thought she was going to faint with excitement.

She sold us a small, wooden nest and told us all about "Daddy Bird's duties" during the time we would be pacing the hospital corridor.

Seems Daddy Bird has to put in equal time on the nest. The birds having already ironed out this male-female liberation thing.

The bird lady said we should continue talking to them in soothing terms. "Compliment Daddy Bird and Mommy Bird equally," she said.

Well, I was not about to address them as Daddy Bird and Mommy Bird. I had already named them "Clarence" and "Stupid," and that was that.

However, it was easy to be fair and equal with the compliments. Mainly because, I didn't have the slightest idea which one was the daddy and which one was the momma.

In due time, there were seven eggs in the nest. And, finally, one day, they all hatched.

A few weeks later, I took the nine parakeets and their cage out on the patio so we could spray inside the house.

A stray football in the back yard knocked over the cage and it fell open.

All nine parakeets flew away in formation without saying a word in parting.

PART THREE

See how orderly things can go when you divide a book into parts.

Sin Along the River

It was on the edge of Sacramento, along the banks of the American River, that I spent my Tom Sawyer years. It was the river where gold was discovered, and I have nothing but golden memories of it.

To reach the river, which was about a mile from our government housing development cottage, it was necessary to cut through the Chinese truck gardens. Big fields of corn and cantaloupes on the vine.

We always arrived at the river with groceries.

While the cantaloupes cooled in the shallow water near our favorite swimming hole, we went hunting with an old single-shot .22 rifle I owned.

We hunted for pheasant or quail, regardless of what time of year it might be. Seasons did not matter to us. As far as we were concerned, we were the last living boys on earth.

Actually, we seldom found pheasant or quail. But we could always find some kind of bird, and figured if one kind of bird was good to eat, so were the rest.

I've dined on many woodpeckers along the banks of the American.

When we got our bird cleaned and the coals of our campfire ready, we would pack the bird in a ball of blue clay dug from the riverbank. Then we would cover it with coals.

Next, we would take our corn, still in husks, and soak it in the water. Then we popped it in the fire.

Now it was time to lean back, smoke a Bull Durham cigarette, and talk of football, girls and soldiering.

When the bird was baked and the corn was steamed, we would break the hardened clay and peel back the hot husks and sit down to our meal.

No salt, no pepper, no butter, but they were the most delicious meals you could imagine.

After the main courses, we would pull our cantaloupes out of the cool water and break them open with our hands

I doubt if the gods ever had sweeter juices running down their chins.

The rest of the afternoon would be spent swimming in forbidden waters. (We were supposed to be at the municipal pool under the watchful eyes of lifeguards.)

Of course, all of these things were wrong. And, perhaps, that was the very reason we so enjoyed them.

We walked home at the end of the day, warmly wrapped in our first sins.

Howling at the Moon

A full moon rises this evening, right in the middle of Dog Days. I told the children: "I may grow some hair on my face tonight, but don't worry. Just hang a sprig of wild garlic on your door, and don't forget to say your prayers."

They said: "Don't *talk* like that! We'll have bad dreams."

I don't really terrify them. That's not nice. (But it's okay to keep them on edge a little bit.)

Dog Days runs from July 3 to Aug. 11. The dictionary calls it "a sultry part of the summer supposed to occur during the period that Sirius, the Dog Star, rises at the same time as the sun."

It's also supposed to be the time for werewolves to come out.

I told the children: "Don't worry. I wouldn't turn into a wolf. Probably the most I would turn into would be a cocker spaniel, or maybe just a poodle."

The cats looked at me with sultry eyes.

"On the other hand," I said, "Maybe I will just grow a beard."

When the weather gets sultry like this, there is no way to get a good night's sleep. The humidity matches the temperature, and the tempers rise.

I got up about 3 a.m., hot and thirsty.

"What's wrong?" asked the wife.

"Nothing," I said. "I'm just going to get a drink of water. I can't sleep."

She said: "Now I don't know if I can go back to sleep."

I dozed off for a little while. Then she got up.

I said: "What's wrong with you?"

She said: "You made me thirsty. I've been lying there thinking about a drink of water."

Whatever happened to sleeping porches? It seems I remember them from some years of my boyhood. When Dog Days arrived, everybody would move out on the cots on the big screened porches.

There was more of a breeze out there, and the night blooming jasmine, breathed deeply, would help sleep to come.

Next morning the children said they couldn't sleep, either. I said! "It's because these are Dog Days."

They said: "Really? Could we get a dog?"

You don't have to turn into a werewolf, or even a poodle. But these are good days to go out and howl at the moon.

A real cowboy told me that. He's a writer now, but he'll always be a real cowboy too.

He said: "You would be surprised how much good it does for your soul to go outside and rare back and really howl at the moon. Try it sometime."

Well, a big city is not the best place to go out and howl at the moon. I mean, there's a mental ward only a few blocks from where I live, and I imagine that would get me a free ride.

However, I have done it.

Last Easter Week, we were vacationing in a cabin fairly high in the Sierra. It was pretty deserted, too. The nearest constable was probably 10 miles away.

One evening I grabbed a young nephew by the arm and said, "C'mon Tony, we're going to go out and howl at the moon. It's good for you." (We had had some refreshments earlier.)

So we walked out into the pines, about 200 yards from the cabin and I let loose at the moon. A high, mournful howl. Then the boy did the same thing.

As we walked back to the cabin, he said: "Gee, Uncle John, that does make you feel better, y'know?"

And it certainly did.

The Torture Trail

Since a little torture never hurt anyone, I agreed to take three teen-age daughters shopping the other afternoon. (Some people just stay home and hit themselves over the head with a hammer. It's the same thing.)

"We just want you to drive us," they said. "We won't take very long."

I said: "Yeah, and it doesn't snow much in Alaska. What do you want to shop for?"

"Mom's birthday present." (Bam! And the Clay Pigeon is tagged on the first shot.)

They said: "We think we can find what we want at that import store down the hill."

I said: "What do you want?"

They said: "We don't know, but we ought to be able to find *something* there."

An hour later at the import store—"Do *you* see anything you think she would like?"

I said: "Well, there are some teakwood monkeys over there. Or, have you thought about a snake skin walking cane?"

They said: "Be serious."

"Maybe we can find something in Old Town," one of them said.

"Yeah, they've got a *lot* of shops there," said another.

(And yet another of us was heard to moan softly.)

Two hours later in Old Town—"Let's go back to that first store and look at those gowns again."

Three hours later in Old Town—"Do you think I should try on that blue blouse?" "I don't know. It doesn't seem right for you."

At this point, I left the entourage and decided to sit down and rest in the shade of a small Mexican restaurant and audition a small Margarita.

Thirty minutes later, I got up and joined them as they walked by. I don't think they even realized I had been gone.

(Confucius said it: "It is admirable for man to take son fishing, but there is special place in heaven for father who takes daughter shopping.")

Four hours later: "Dad, we're ready to go now. We finally got everything we need."

I said: "Thank heavens. We've probably already missed supper, and my feet are killing me."

On the way home they said: "You don't really like going shopping with us too much, do you dad?"

I said: "It's better than sticking needles up my fingernails."

Toward the Bend of the River

Summer days in the high Sierra. The aspen are beginning to turn gold. The late afternoon breeze sends blue campfire smoke twisting through the big trees.

By tomorrow I hope to have my portable typewriter set up beside a small fork of the Kaweah River.

I plan to interview several trout on this trip.

I may even take a pie pan and discover a little gold.

Then again, I may just lie under a tree most of the time and discover a little silence. (Which, as Thomas Carlyle pointed out, is also golden.)

This is the land of the sequoia tree, the giant named for the great Indian scholar who invented the Cherokee alphabet.

Teddy Roosevelt loved this tree so much, he made it against the law for man to even pick up and move a dead chunk of it.

It takes 2,000 years to grow a big one.

The children want to camp at a bend in the stream where the rumbling trout truck parks two afternoons a week to dump a load of rainbows fresh from the hatchery.

These fish arrive in a bad mental condition. The ride from the hatchery gives them what amounts to the blind staggers.

They reel around in the stream bed, and will bite on anything. (Kids catch them on small gold hooks that they don't even bother to bait.)

It is considered very bad form for an adult to go after the stoned fish.

(That's okay. I have enough children to catch supper.)

After a half hour, if the fish is not in somebody's creel, his hangover goes away and he shoots up or down stream.

This country is dotted with lakes, too. The trout in them are planted from airplanes. The pilot swoops down low, and the finger-length fish are pushed out the door.

No parachutes, either. Geronimo!

There is more to the day up in this country. The summer sunlight lasts about an hour longer here. It's just a matter of being farther north.

But the valleys are in shade almost an hour before the last bit of sunlight slips off the higher peaks.

And as evening settles in, the smells of wood smoke and black coffee ride the air mingled with the flavor of pine and wild mint.

It's climbing country, too. A lot of fair-sized mountains to work out on. As it begins to get dark, the young climbers gather around their campfires, play guitars and harmonicas, and sing long into the night.

They are joined by crickets and night birds.

It's a soft, beautiful symphony under a million stars.

AWOOHOOOO!

You see more of this Golden State when you travel with eight children in the car. This is because you have occasion to stop more.

I have been thinking of writing a guidebook with recommendations on the restrooms along Highway 99. So far as I know, I haven't missed any between San Diego and Sacramento.

I said: "But we just stopped about 15 minutes ago. Why didn't you go then?"

The child said: "I didn't need to then."

The service stations north of the Tehachapis are huge cases for the traveling family. Besides the gas pumps and restrooms, each is equipped with large banks of coin machines offering everything from soft drinks to peanut butter sandwiches. One child heads for the restroom, and a half dozen others run for the machines. (I can get by with less pocket change in Las Vegas.)

I am pretty sure that the average child would rather have a spinach sandwich than a T-bone steak, if he could get the sandwich out of a machine.

The human animal seems to be born with an instinct to put coins in slots and pull handles or push buttons. And I am surprised that science hasn't been given a grant to look into it.

The second section of my guidebook will deal with foods that you should not attempt to eat while driving with those eight children.

Number one on this list, I think, will be cottage cheese. There are few things more distracting than, after being forced to brake sharply, driving the rest of the trip with a glob of cottage cheese down the back of your neck.

Sliced tomatoes also will have a high priority. They get down the backs of seats, on the floorboard; I have even found them in the ashtrays. They rarely get into the child. Add to this chilidogs, Chinese food, tacos, goopy burgers and anything else that is more likely to drip down the outside than the inside of offspring.

And I might include almost all liquids, except for a minimum amount of water (just enough to keep the child alive) for reasons explained in the restroom section of the book. My wife thinks I would have children starve and go thirsty while motoring.

My wife is right.

The third and final section of my guidebook will deal with children's games which should not be played in the car.

This list includes a variety of well-known sports such as wrestling, football and any variety of catch.

However, there is an even longer list of lesser known activities which should be strictly forbidden.

Some of these are: "He hit me first," "Let's see who can take up most of the seat," "Let's all sing a different song at the same time," and that ever-popular "Let's make a motion with our arms and get the guy driving the monstrous diesel alongside us to blow his air horn."

We are camped today in a place called Cold Springs, 7,000 feet into the Sierras. Whoever named the place was an honest man.

We took a slight dip in the stream yesterday. By slight, I mean like a 10th of a second. I would guess the water temperature is a good three or four degrees. Madre Mia!

However, it is the sweetest, purest water you can find. It turns black coffee into an experience. And I cannot describe the wonders it does to a little splash of snake bite medicine around the evening campfire.

As I write this, there are four rainbow trout lying side by side in a nearby frying pan, each wrapped snugly with a strip of bacon.

The pancakes are turning a golden brown.

There are fresh slices of melon, chilled during the night in the stream bed.

And I cannot help feeling sorry for everybody in the world but us right now.

Still, it is not bliss every moment in these mountains. Last night we were visited by a couple of hungry bears. I have never heard such frightening noises in my life.

Not from the bears. From my wife.

There are about 20 other families camped here. Every morning the topic of conversation is about what the bears did the previous night.

"They got all our bacon," said the young couple camped just below us. "Did they do any damage to you people."

I said: "A little. They wiped out one trash bag and my wife's composure."

This morning my first job was to check all the sleeping bags to make sure the bears had not carried away any of the children.

I said: "Bears don't have a taste for children. They like things like bacon and cookies and flour. Children taste terrible to them."

She said: "Tonight everybody is sleeping inside the tent. They could be stepped on or something."

That ought to be cozy. We only started this trip with eight children. And, just to make sure they wouldn't be lonely, we picked up a couple of young cousins in Visalia.

I said: "The chances of a bear actually hurting a human are a million to one."

She said: "I don't like the odds."

Despite the nightly bears, this is a marvelous place to be. We are in the shadows of giant sequoia trees, sugarpine and conifer. And the air smells like it must have vitamins in it. There are more than a dozen lakes within hiking distance from our camp. This afternoon three of our boys plan to walk up to Eagle Lake, about two miles away.

There are tales of huge brown trout up there, and the boys intend to check them out ("Watch out for bears," said their mother).

A couple of the girls are going to walk downstream and look for wild berries. They have decided the bend in the stream where all the Boy Scouts are camped would be an excellent place to search for berries.

The wife is going to do the family wash in the dish pan. Her dryer is a small silvertip pine near the tent, and it looks like the most unusually decorated Christmas tree in the world when she gets all the clothes on it.

And your pine scented correspondent plans to sit out here in my Redwood-paneled office and do battle with the old portable typewriter.

It's a tough life, but I think I can take it.

The Three Bears and Yellowlocks

Once upon a time, in the deep dark forest, lived three bears. Possibly they were a mama bear, a papa bear and a baby bear. But no one had enough courage to get out of their sleeping bags and take a look.

Into this forest one day came a small golden-haired girl, who carried with her a basket of cookies and corned beef and eggs, a husband, assorted children, a tent, camp stoves, fire permits, fishing poles, and a lot of things like that.

We will call this girl Yellowlocks, for they were. And so was she, when it came to bears. (Which it came to, indeed.)

The deep forest where these bears lived, and where Yellowlocks went to camp and rest and wash dishes outdoors, was called Sequoia National forest.

It was named this because of the giant sequoia trees there.

And if you think the sequoia trees are big, you should see the bears. (No one did. But Yellowlocks, having been to college, made an educated guess that they were probably 40 feet tall.) At first, Yellowlocks did not even know there were bears in the forest. She heard some strange noises the first night, but figured they were probably just lions or tigers. So she zipped up the tent flap and went fast asleep. (Not too fast, though.)

The next morning, Yellowlocks got out of bed, walked over to the table, and said: "Somebody's been eating my trash, and ate it all up."

"Oh," said a lady from a nearby camp who happened to be walking by on her way to a small wooden building. "That would be the three bears. We have three bears in this camp. They come around every night looking for food. Don't leave food out, my dear. And sometimes you can scare them away by banging on pans."

Yellowlocks sat down and drank eight cups of coffee, some of which she spilt because it was hard to drink hot coffee and bang on a pan at the same time.

Pretty soon her husband got up and walked out of the tent.

"Oh," said Yellowlocks, "I thought you were going to sleep in this morning, dear."

Her husband said: "I found it difficult to do with you banging on the pans like that. Have you lost your mind?"

She said: "Certainly not, I am keeping the bears away."

Her husband said: "I don't see any bears."

Yellowlocks said: "You may thank me for that."

Bang . . . bang . . .

"Is there any more coffee?" asked her husband, shaking his head to get the ringing out of his ears.

"No," said Yellowlocks, "but I will make some more right away. While I'm doing that, will you check the tent to see if any of the children have been eaten up?"

After he had a couple of cups of coffee—and Yellowlocks had about six more—her husband tried to explain to her that the bears would not eat anybody up, but were just lazy national forest type bears who preferred to live off the fat of the land. "So don't leave any fat out," he said.

"Yes, dear," said Yellowlocks. Bang . . . bang . . .

That afternoon, the entire family went down to the stream to bathe and fish and cool off. "Hand me my rod," said one of the children. "Hand me my pan," said Yellowlocks.

"Good grief," said her husband. "You aren't going to take that pan to the stream, are you?" Yellowlocks said: "You have your trusty scout knife. I have my trusty pan." Bang . . . bang . . .

That night everybody went to bed in the tent and the car. And the bears came. (In one way, it was a good thing they did. Otherwise, everybody would have lain there with their eyes open all night long for nothing.)

Clatter clang . . . went the garbage cans up the road, as the bears rummaged through them.

"Do you suppose they could rip the doors off the car?" whispered Yellowlocks. Bang . . . bang . . .

"I think they're coming closer," whispered Yellowlocks. Bang . . . bang . . . "Hail Mary, full of grace," prayed Yellowlocks. Bang . . . bang . . .

The bears hung around the camp for about an hour, making noises which were indeed frightening. And the next morning, Yellowlocks grabbed up her basket, and children, and husband and things, and headed down the hills and out of the forest as fast as she could.

(And so did a lot of other people, who were not particularly afraid of bears. But they couldn't stand the constant pan banging all night long.)

Getting Out of the Woods

We drove down out of the Sierras, hugging the inside of the narrow ribbon of road. Honking the horn at every blind bend.

I looked over the cliff edge. It looked like a two-day fall.

My wife's right hand, clutching the arm rest, was turning white.

I said: "It's certainly awesome scenery, isn't it?"

She said: "I refuse to open my eyes."

That's gratitude for you. I drive 500 miles, sleep on the hard ground, shave in cold water, and have my bacon eaten by the bears, just to show her some of the most spectacular scenery ever sculpted by God and Nature.

And she refuses to look at it.

I said: "Keeping your eyes closed isn't what's keeping us on the road."

She said: "I can't help it. I simply can't stand to look down there. Tell me when we get to level ground."

Halfway down the mountain, we stopped at a place called the Indian Baths. (I think the boys and I named it ourselves a few years ago. I've never heard anybody else call it that. But it looks like a place where Indians might have taken baths.)

A vein of granite about 40-feet wide and running hundreds of yards down the mountain side. A sheet of cold spring water about an inch deep pouring down it.

Except, here and there a few feet apart are potholes about the size and depth of a bathtub. A natural Jacuzzi, carved in stone.

The granite, where the water runs over it so thin is slick as greased glass. The kids love to climb up and slide down, splashing with glee here and there into one of the potholes.

Sort of like the old Shoot-the-Chute rides.

(The kids go down fully clothed in jeans and shirts to prevent rock burns. I shudder to think of the Indians in their breech cloths.)

After the Indian Baths, the road straightens out slightly, but it drops sharply and the searing heat of the valley hits you hard.

(Not the kids, though. They are still soaking wet, and comfortable.)

Down into California's sprawling breadbasket, the Great Central Valley. Fruit stands, "Fresh Eggs For Sale" signs, lemon groves, and bait stands dot Highway 198.

Up over the Tehachapis—the Ridge Route or Grapevine. At the top, near Lebec, we got the first breath of cool Southern California air in a week.

We stopped in a little town we didn't even know existed—Frazier Park. It's three miles off the road, and I always thought it was a park. It turned out to be a little village isolated in the mountains.

I don't have any idea why it's there.

We had sandwiches, hard-boiled eggs and lemonade under a shady oak near the heart of town, and rested our road-weary muscles. (My shoulders were about shot from that mountain road.)

I said: "I dread getting started again. We've still got that L.A. traffic."

She said: "I don't know why it bothers you so. I'll be glad to drive."

I said: "Okay. I'll keep my eyes closed."

A No-Strings Dog

Up in the cool gray morning with Fred, the neighbor's dog. We both are stirring around in the kitchen before the sun comes over the garage.

I get up to light the faulty hot water heater. Otherwise, we would be shaving and showering in ice water.

Fred gets up and drops by just in case I would like to have company for breakfast.

"Good morning, neighbor!" he barks. "Boy, I am *starving,* aren't you? Here, have a last lick from a starving dog!"

This dog can play the heartstrings like a virtuoso. (I'll bet he gets three or four breakfasts a day around the neighborhood with that act.)

I said: "Sit down, Fred, while I fix coffee."

I said: "Fred, why don't you go down to the Old Globe Theater next time they have auditions. I think you are probably a natural actor."

Fred wiggles and trembles and shakes with emotion all over. It's been a whole night since he's had a meal!

He barks: "Hey, can I do anything to help! Can I help you look in the refrigerator? Can I lick your hand while you look?"

We are between dogs this summer. Plenty of other pet stock around. Cats, hamsters, birds, fish, and such.

However, we do not have a completely fenced yard. Therefore, no dog of our own.

Fred is aware of this, and does what he can to help. He drops by to visit at least three times a day. Breakfast, lunch, and dinner.

Also, knowing how much we like dogs, he often brings a few friends by with him. He'll stand there, backed up by a couple of shaggy buddies, and bark a few times by way of introduction. Then, he'll wag his tail and smile.

I said: "Fred, nothing personal, but you sure hang around with a weird crowd."

These are "no strings attached" dogs. We can romp with them in the yard, throw sticks, and pet them. But we do not have to be responsible for them running loose.

Still, I suppose if Fred got busted and called in the middle of the night, I'd scrape up his bail.

I have never seen a collar or a tag on Fred. I have always assumed he lived just up the street. But, maybe not. (Maybe the neighbor thinks he is my dog.)

Recently, we took a little trip up north and Fred wagged goodbye from the driveway.

When we returned a week later, there was Fred. Standing there, looking thin and quizzical.

As if to say, "Where have you guys *been?* I thought you were just going to the *store,* or something."

I pulled a pound of raw hamburger out of the camp cooler, and Fred got every bit of it down in three gulps.

Then he ran around in circles in the yard, stopping now and then to lick somebody, then shooting off again. He dived into a bush, scared a bird, then rushed back to tell us about it.

And, just to add a special little touch of appreciation, he went out and dug us a dog hole in the middle of the yard.

I don't know. Maybe we aren't between dogs after all this summer.

The Last Practical Joker

Somewhere during the past 25 years, the business of living became such a deadly serious thing that an early bit of Americana all but disappeared.

I am talking about the practical joke. Whatever happed to it?

I don't mean simple little stunts. I am referring to the truly elaborate, well-conceived practical joke. The kind that some-times took weeks, or even months, to pull off.

A friend I once had named Bob was one of the best practition-ers of this unique art form that I ever ran across.

I think the thing that delighted me so much about Bob's stunts was the fact that they never hurt anyone. When the joke was over, the victim never even realized it had happened.

The stunt was strictly for Bob's own amusement.

Bob had his little spur-of-the-moment jokes, too. One of his favorites was approaching a drunk panhandler on lower K Street in Sacramento. Bob would stagger up to the glassy-eyed moocher and demand: "Shay, thish ish my side of the street. Get over on your own side."

The confused drunk, in no condition to argue with anyone, would reel to the corner and cross the street.

Bob, meanwhile, would jaywalk and approach the drunk again on the other side. "I told you thish was my side of the street. Will you get the hell on the other side?"

The drunk would shake his head in disbelief, and reel once again to the corner. Bob would cross again in the middle of the block.

Three or four times of this and the drunk, unable to cope with that kind of unreality, would stumble homeward. And Bob would stand there with a little gleam in his eyes.

But a classic example of Bob's patience involved a joke that lasted an entire year while he was serving in the Army. At first, it may sound a little cruel, but the victim never even knew about it, and probably doesn't to this day.

In Bob's barracks one day came a tall, gangling young private from Tennessee. A soft-spoken, kind boy, but somewhat limited in education. He was literate, but barely.

Bob became friends with Arthur from Tennessee, and they went to base movies and the PX together. Bob, who had traveled all over the world, posed as a country boy just like Arthur. He talked of crops and horses and good home whiskey. And Arthur never doubted the fabricated background for a minute.

One day Bob told Arthur that he was feeling "just dang miserable" because he'd like to write his girlfriend back home, but he unfortunately could neither read nor write.

Arthur, friend that he was said: "Heck, Bob, I kin write a little. I'd write your letters for you."

From then on, Bob would dictate a letter to his imaginary girlfriend every Friday night.

At first, they were simple little "I am fine—how are you?" notes. But gradually, very gradually, Bob began using bigger words.

"How do you spell 'excellent,' Bob?" Arthur would ask. "Golly, don't ask me," Bob would say.

Toward the end of the year, Bob was dictating sentences such as, "A pernicious new lieutenant in our outfit is trying to usurp the authority of Colonel Walker's aide-de-camp. But, c'est la guerre!"

The sentence would boggle Arthur's mind, and Bob would feign total ignorance of how such words are put together.

When they parted company for new assignments, Arthur went away completely unaware of what had happened. But he was never hurt by the gag. He had had a good friend for a year. And his vocabulary had increased considerably.

Bob himself disappeared one night during a patrol on Guam. I think he took the practical joke with him.

Model A Memories

It was a quiet Sunday afternoon, and we were sitting around the living room going through old photographs.

"You mean that was your first car?" said one of my teen-age sons. "Wow, what a bummer!"

I said: "That car was *not* a bummer. That car was a perfectly acceptable Model A which Mr. Henry Ford sold to me, used, for $125."

He said: "Did it run good?"

I said: "It ran—usually. I admit it often had to be pushed to get it started, and a good many young ladies in long gowns developed better shoulder muscles during the two years I had it. But that was all perfectly acceptable in a Model A back then."

He said: "You mean you made your dates help push it?"

I said: "You might say I *allowed* them to push in emergency cases. Otherwise, *nobody* touched that car but me, unless they were wearing white gloves."

I loved that car. It had a leak in the radiator and in one of the tires, a slightly cracked block, and a broken handle on the rumble seat.

But it also had a brush-paint job of bright turquoise, a whitewall spare, and a set of musical horns that I could play "Sabre Dance" on. In other words, it was a class vehicle.

This was in Sacramento, about a thousand years ago, I think. I forget now where I got the $125 to buy that car, for I rarely made a gasoline purchase bigger than 60 cents. (And I recall some as small as 18 cents, but that was a full gallon then.)

The gas gauge on my Model A did not work, but it hardly mattered. Under the seat I kept a 12-inch ruler. All I had to do was take the gas cap off, and stick the ruler in.

The part that came out wet showed me how much gas was left.

The car hood opened from the side—both sides. They hooked down. But the engine was so unpredictable, I rarely fastened the hooks.

Also, the emergency brake did not work. But I carried a couple of bricks to put under the wheels.

You had to be resourceful in those days.

Because gas money was so scarce in those days, whenever we came to a hill, we would turn off the key and coast down in neutral. A free ride.

There was one hill, Meyer's Grade, on the highway from

Sacramento to the south side of Lake Tahoe—back in the days when Stateline was one restaurant half in Nevada and half in California. (You ate on one side, and walked across the room to play the slot machines.)

Meyer's Grade was eight-miles up and eight-miles down. It took us half an hour to climb the thing, but we passed every car on the road coming down.

And we took the downhill run without a penny's worth of gas. Whoooosh. Silently around the curves, with just a slight touch of brakes now and then.

The people we passed must have thought we had some new kind of secret engine.

"Yep, it was quite a car," I told my son. "A perfect blending of young man and young machine. Nothing like today's super sports bombs that turn parents and insurance salesmen white."

"It sounds neat," he said.

We put the photograph away, and the strains of "Sabre Dance" faded back into the past.

Yours Truly, the Computer

Almost into August and we still haven't run out of June weather. Hazy at the beach. Too humid to do much more than lie around in the hammock and read a book.

During a slight fit of insanity, I joined a book club the other day. Lured by a membership offer of about $60 worth of books for $1.

I don't know why I do these things. I was on that merry-go-round once before. It took me years to get off.

The offer sounds simple enough. All I have to do is buy four books a year, then I can resign my membership.

It's trickier than that, though. You do not request the book-of-the-month. You can only request *not* to get it.

"Return this card within such and such time if you do not want the current selection."

"Such and such time" is a period behavioral scientists have

figured out that is just *short* of the time the average man will get around to returning the card.

The books keep coming. The bills keep coming. The house takes on a fine literary air. And pretty soon I am in hock up to here.

I kept trying to resign from the last book company. I wrote letter after letter. "Get me *out* of this chicken outfit," I said. (That was one of my later letters. I was getting pretty heated up.)

Trouble was, there was no one in the company to listen to me. I don't think there were any *people* in the company at all. It was completely run by machines.

Printing presses and computers.

The computer got my letter, digested it, and whirred out instructions to the press: "Send-this-subject-form-letter-33B4-and-bill-$18.27."

I moved a couple of times and put in change of address cards. I wrote a friendly letter to the computer, but it never got the message.

Now, by the time the cards that should be returned if I didn't want the books got to me, it was two days past the deadline to return them.

Man, were we getting books.

I wired the computer. Apparently the computer wasn't programmed to take wires.

I got a phone call from one of the computer's henchmen early one morning from New York. He said: "Now, about your bill."

I said: "Excuse me for interrupting, but could you give me the time?"

He said: "Sure, it's 8:15."

I said: "Well, that's just splendid. I hope you're having a sunny morning in New York. Do you know what the hell time it is in California?" (Click.)

Finally, I sent a letter in the computer's own language. I wrote:

"Dear Computer: Look, I insist you take me off your membership rolls. It is useless to keep sending me books and bills, for I am a computer, too. And I am not programmed to read them, and I am not programmed to pay them, and I do not have any money, anyway.

"You can take me to court if you want to, but I weigh 17,000 pounds. Sincerely, JO8NS1NOR, Model 5-9."

True story.

Mother's Birthday Suit

We chalked off another year over the weekend. I whispered to the girls: "Do you want to run to the store for some cake mix?" They whispered back: "We're making a homemade one."

Then they said aloud: "*Mother,* you're *not* supposed to be listening!"

I went out and bought a lot of daffy cards. I don't think anybody's *ever* gotten a serious card in this family.

We buy the kind that says things like: "Before opening this card, close one eye to get the full effect."

On the inside, it says: "You *did* it! You actually closed one eye! Boy, what a ninny! Now I wished I'd told you to tear off all your clothes and run around the room in circles singing grand opera!"

Happy birthday.

I tiptoed out of the bedroom at 7 on birthday morning. It's a standard birthday present. She gets to sleep in late. But that's difficult when it comes on Saturday.

I said: "Turn those cartoons down. Your mother's still asleep."

We went shopping for a bathing suit. Another present. She said: "Maybe I ought to buy a one-piece suit this year. I still would like to lose five pounds."

I said: "I read somewhere that a bikini is actually more complimentary to a fat person than a one-piecer."

She said: "I didn't say anything about *fat,* I said five pounds." (And she said it rather coolly, I might add.)

I said: "Who's talking about you? I was just making a general statement. (Whew! The general almost stepped on a land mine that time.)

She settled on a *three* piece bathing suit. A bikini underneath, and a vest like thing that buckles in front and covers the other two pieces.

That way, she can make her decision at the beach.

The birthday chick has a little weird twist about her. She doesn't actually lie about her age. She just gets mixed up about it.

In a few weeks, she will get to thinking how old she will be on her *next* birthday. That will play on her mind for awhile. Then she'll begin telling people that's her age.

A Michigan professor studied birthdays and found that most women who lie about their age, subtract an even 10 years.

But mine goes around most the time, telling people she is a year older than she actually is. (I guess it's a pleasant surprise every birthday to find you've lost a year instead of gained one.)

On the way home from the shopping trip, I said: "Look, before we go home to the cake and the kids' presents, let's stop someplace quiet and I'll buy you a birthday toast."

The bar where we stopped was fairly dark, and she barely makes it over five feet tall.

The man at the door asked her: "Could I see some I.D. please?"

It was probably the nicest birthday present of all.

Backstage at the Beauty Pageant

Blue skies returned after a mid-summer thunder and lightning storm. (Wow! I woke up thinking I was in Indiana!)

This is National Smile Week. Stand up straight and smile, people.

It is also National Beauty Queen Week. (Smile at a beauty queen. Kill two birds.)

I used to interview (and smile at) beauty queens. Miss Cranberry. Miss Outboard Motor. Miss Raisin. Miss Pickle Packer, Miss Flame—a hot number named by the fire department.

The interviews were nothing startling.

"What would you like to be, Miss Dairy Queen?"

"I would like to be a model or an actress."

"How do you feel about being named Miss Pickle Packer, Miss Pickle Packer?"

"It's been a wonderful experience. All the other girls are just wonderful. I'm just having a wonderful time."

Like I say, not much depth in the material. But the pictures always made front page.

I told my wife about the days I had to cover some of the Miss California preliminaries. I was assigned to the dressing room to get interviews with the girls' mothers.

She said: "You mean you had to go back while they were dressing?"

I said: "Listen, those girls were so far up on cloud nine, they didn't even notice me."

She said: "How about *you*? Were *you* on cloud nine too?"

I said: "Look, I'm a journalist. It's like being a doctor, you know?"

(Sometimes I have to do some of my most creative writing during these breakfast table conversations.).

She said: "I'll bet."

I said: "It's National Smile Week. Smile."

Anyway, about these queen mothers. The ones I ran into were pretty strange.

I mean, their daughters may have been sitting around in a trance with glazed eyes. But the mamas knew *exactly* what was happening.

They knew which judge favored which *other* girl. (They suspected he was related.)

They knew two or three contestants who couldn't be *that* blonde—naturally.

And they were pretty sure some of the girls weren't *that* size in yesterday's bathing suit rehearsal.

Anyway, it's in the grand American tradition. The beauty

queen contest. Some of the big ones give away fantastic prizes. Trips to Europe. Hollywood screen tests. Wardrobes. A year of wining and dining with the "name" people.

I particularly liked the remark of one former queen after turning over her crown to the new year's winner.

Of beauty contests, she said: "After a year of it, I'm not sure about who are the winners and who are the losers."

Last Day in a Trenchcoat

Got one of those poison pen letters in the mail. "How can you write about such trivia when the world is staggering with important issues?"

It wasn't signed. They almost never are. (The unseen enemy.)

I got a pretty nasty letter from a lady once that *was* signed. I was so delighted that she said what she felt and didn't hide her identity that I wrote her a letter of congratulations.

Then she wrote me a nice letter back. We got to know and like each other. (It takes two people to make a brother.)

Oh well. I threw the most recent letter in the wastebasket. I should worry about one more enemy. I've got them all over the world.

I acquired most of them when I was writing about staggering important issues.

Long ago in another city, they made me a police reporter one day. I went out and bought a trenchcoat and started writing about important issues like murder and such.

I moonlighted by writing stories about murderers for detective magazines.

The stories weren't very complimentary to the murderers. Also, the editors juiced them up with some pretty grisly titles. "The Monster of Modesto." That sort of thing.

Well, all those stories were written only after the murderer had been convicted. But a lot of them only got life sentences.

A life sentence in California means you can be paroled in seven years. I wrote all those stories about 15 years ago.

I figure a lot of those "monsters" are out by now—and probably remember my name.

Sometimes I think about it at night.

The case that shook me up the most was one where the defendant didn't get life. A young man, about 22 I think, who had shot a Fresno bartender.

I was invited to the execution.

(They used to send these formal looking little invitations to the press. They look a little like a wedding invitation.)

The paper said I had to go. (In the old days, some papers used to think that was a great front page story. A step by step account of a man's last steps.)

I went. Crossed the gray bay by auto ferry to the gray walls of San Quentin Prison.

I won't describe what I saw, but I saw it. I also ran into the boy's mother outside the prison afterwards.

I came home, gave my trenchcoat to the Salvation Army, quit my job, and wrote a letter to San Diego.

I said: "I've always wanted to live by the sea. Do you need a writer to write about flowers or children or pets or any of the other unimportant things in life?"

The King of August

Grass has been growing like Oklahoma corn around here lately. The very heat that makes it unbearable to push a lawnmower around also makes the grass shoot up like teenagers.

I said: "I'm going to *have* to mow it. It's getting to be a fire hazard."

Well, I did not cut *just* the grass.

I also cut a screwdriver, a spoon, a plastic boat, and three playing cards. The rotary blades also sent a small rubber ball flying over the fence into the neighbor's yard.

I shouted: "Why can't people pick things up? Who left all this stuff out here?"

No answer.

I didn't expect one without a little evidence. Never in my life has a child stepped forward and said to me: "Sir, I did it."

If I can *prove* they did it, that's a different story. But we're short on George Washingtons around here.

There is a big spreading pepper tree in the back yard. A table under the tree. A doll house on the table. This attracts little neighborhood dolls from up and down the street.

I was stopped by a little moppet in shorts and long blond hair in my driveway.

"Hi"

I said: "Hi, yourself."

"Where you going?"

I said: "To the store."

"Why?"

I said: "To get some things."

"What things?" (This kid should be hired by the force. What an interrogator!)

I said: "What's your name, honey?"

"Victah."

I guess that's Victor. But I would have sworn the kid was a female, with all those questions.)

Under the spreading pepper tree, the village wordchopper went to sleep the other night. It was so blasted hot in the house, I just sacked out in the hammock.

Now a pepper tree, as you may know, sheds. Leaves and tiny little flowers about the size of confetti.

After a few hours, I guess I was pretty well covered with a sort of a summer snow. But I didn't realize it.

Sometime in the middle of the night, after it had cooled off, I got out of the hammock and stumbled upstairs to bed.

The next morning the wife said: "What happened? How come the bed's full of weeds? How come *you're* full of weeds? Look at your hair in the mirror?"

I squinted at the mirror. Little pepper tree blossoms all through my hair.

I said: "Those aren't weeds. They're flowers. I'm the king of August. Go back to sleep."

The Elephant Rider

A clock radio came on down the hall. Loud rock at 7 o'clock. I shouted down the hall: "Shut that thing off!"

It wrecked a good dream I was in. I wanted to see how it turned out. I dream nothing but high adventure dreams. Cinerama and color by Technicolor.

"Don't wake me up till I run out of dreams," I said.

The wife got up. "I've got a million things to do today, anyway," she said. "We're behind on laundry. There's Monica's swimming lesson. I've got to call the doctor."

She said: "Are you going into the office today?"

I said: "Of course. I have to go in. I've got a million things to do down there."

She said: "What do you have to do besides write the column?"

I said: "That's not fair. You only named three of your million. Besides, what do you have to call the doctor for?"

She said: "I want to get another prescription for that throat medicine. I also have to go to the bank. That's another thing."

I said: "Well, I have to make arrangements about riding an elephant."

She said: "What elephant? What in the world are you talking about?"

I said: "Well, I sort of promised I would ride an elephant on opening night of the circus for the COMBO benefit."

She said: "Really?" She started giggling.

I said: "What's so funny? It's for a good cause. Besides, it's the kind of thing newspapermen do all the time."

She said: "I know. I just can't picture you riding around on an elephant. What kind of arrangements do you have to make?"

I said: "How do I know? I've never ridden an elephant. Maybe they want me to practice or something. Maybe they just want to introduce me to the elephant. I don't guess you just hop on a strange elephant and start riding him around."

The kids got word of this at the breakfast table. They went out and told all the other kids on the block. The other kids came around.

They said: "Are you *really* going to ride an elephant in the circus?"

I said: "Sure. Nothing to it. Just hop up there and ride the old brute around center ring a few times. Giddap, elephant!"

They said: "Gee."

I went in and told the wife: "That's another thing. I've got to figure out some kind of outfit to wear."

She said: "To wear where?"

I said: "While riding the elephant, of course. You don't expect me to appear in Ringling Brothers and Barnum and Bailey Circus wearing a grey business suit, do you?"

She said: "Maybe I could sew some sequins on Katie's ballet tights."

I said: "Don't be cute. And stop that silly giggling."

(It's pitiful how little women understand of the varied responsibilities of the American businessman.)

Sailing into September this week. Everybody back to school. The wife back to work. Clear the deck! (The deck being clear, I can start writing at home again.)

A nasty letter in the morning mail. Unsigned, as usual. (Oh boy, that gets to me. Nothing they can say is as nasty as the fact they are afraid to say who said it.)

"Why do you let your wife work? I raise a big family, and my wife doesn't have to work."

Oh boy, oh boy, oh boy!

Dear Anonymous Nut: My wife works because she wants to work. She works in a school for troubled youngsters because she's good at it. If you really have a big family, why don't you show your own wife your letter—especially the part saying "my wife doesn't have to work."

Sorry to start this thing on such a testy note, but unsigned crank letters really crank me up.

Now you know how to really bug me, dear enemies.

Meanwhile, the rest of us will go looking for bluebirds.

Call Me Buffalo John

I grew a mustache, then I started growing a beard. "Why are you growing a mustache and beard?" asked the children. I said: "I have decided to become Buffalo Bill."

They said: "You can't become Buffalo Bill."

I said: "Why not? William Frederick Cody did."

They said: "But his *name* was Bill."

I said: "Okay. I will become Buffalo John. It makes little difference."

Everybody else is growing a beard these days. It started out as a beatnik thing when Jack Kerouac was hanging around the City Lights in San Francisco. Later, it was adopted by the Brooks Brothers bunch.

The beard is very fashionable these days. It gets you better tables at restaurants.

My beard is really a goatee kind of thing. It's still too hot for a full beard.

They said: "How come your chin whiskers are *all* white?"

I said: "That's how I picture Buffalo Bill."

In my downy youth, the beard was frowned upon. If you had a beard, you were a bum. We shaved once a week, and kept our hair trimmed neatly. Crewcuts or big pompadours up front.

The really hard guys let their hair grow long in back, then combed it in the shape of a duck's tail. (Actually, they called it a DA.)

These people were not allowed inside the school dances. They hung around outside, in Model A hot-rods, threatening the freshmen. (The Senior football players were pretty safe.)

Now and then we would try for a little thin-lined mustache.

(Clark Gable was very big then.) After about a week, our mothers would say: "What's that on your lip? Dirt?"

Humiliated, we would head for the bathroom and shave it off.

I said: "I may even get myself a buckskin coat, fringed boots and a wide-brimmed hat."

(In other words, modern dress.)

Not much need for a Buffalo Bill any more. The buffalo are all gone. Except for a few kept as living museum pieces.

Old Bill himself did away with 4,000 of them. Shot them to feed the crews building a railroad across Kansas.

Later, he was saddened at having helped wipe out the Indians' source of life. He said: "How was I to know the damned buffalo reproduced so slowly? Nobody knew that!"

He went into a wild west show and tried to relive his Indian-fighting days in the center ring with makeup on his face.

He was a proud man and liked being a national hero. He had won a Congressional Medal of Honor in 1872 for fighting the Cheyenne.

(Later, somebody mentioned he wasn't eligible for the medal, since he was a civilian. But Congress was nice enough to wait until he died in 1917 before taking it away.)

The children said: "Are you going buffalo hunting?"

I said: "No. From where the sun now stands, I will shoot no more buffalo. But I may join the next wild west show that comes to town."

Up and Down the State

Off to the north over the weekend. (I once swore I would never drive *anywhere* on the Labor Day weekend. When told we *had* to, I swore again.)

"Do you think it will be foggy in San Francisco?" I am asked.

I said: "Why wouldn't it be foggy in San Francisco?"

She said: "Well, we're going to be in the valley part of the time. I don't know *what* to take to wear."

I said: "There's only going to be four of us in the bus. Why don't you just take everything?" (That really would simplify it. There's no agony for this girl worse than a decision.)

We are turning a couple of offspring over to the University of California at Santa Cruz this year. Purpose of the weekend trip was to let them see the campus and their living quarters.

She said: "I wonder if we should take raincoats?"

I said: "For Pete's sake, don't forget the typewriter." (Nothing like having to drive all over California on Labor Day weekend and work at the same time.)

The bus is not exactly a bomb on the road. With all that traffic, I figure it is a little like playing Russian Roulette with four loaded chambers.

However, we had a game plan.

Drive through the desert, cut over to Bakersfield, then up to Visalia where we change ponies. We pick up my sister's Mercedes, turn on the air conditioning, and arrive at UC in style.

I said: "It's a little risky, though. They may cancel their student loans when they see us pull up in a $7,000 automobile."

(If anybody squawked, I figured I could show them the sleeping bags in the trunk and the baloney sandwiches in the cooler.)

We wanted to take the coast route all the way up, but no way, man. Any time I put a couple of curves within five minutes of each other, half the people in this family get car sick.

"Do you feel car sick?" "No, not yet. Do you?"

I said: "For Pete's sake, stop *talking* about it. You're going to talk yourself *into* it."

That's another thing. Every time we put our kids in a car, it turns into an immediate yak session. Everybody talks at once. Nobody listens to anybody else. And when they get tired of talking, they sing.

This tends to shred the driver's nerves. (Mother says: "Now, everybody hush for awhile. It's very hard driving in all this traffic." Then they start "Shhhhing" anybody who begins to open his mouth. They "Shhhh" louder than they talk.)

I once tried to invent a little game to create silence. I said I would give a penny for every minute of silence, but I would take it back from the guy who talked.

Nobody got very rich.

Autumn days in the great Salinas Valley. There is the smell of harvest in the Pastures of Heaven. But times are changing.

John Steinbeck might get lost if he were alive today to roam these rolling hills.

You can still buy 25 artichokes for a dollar. But artichoke land is being choked out by development dollars. And the fruit orchards to the east are growing smaller every year.

Still a big chunk of farm country, though, and you can taste the farmer's wares at countless big and little stands along all roads that aren't freeways.

A dozen or more vineyards also have tasting rooms among these hills. The big names, like Almaden and Maisson, and many smaller ones.

An hour on the roads around here and you can be driving around in a rosy glow.

We stopped at a big one. Casa de Fruta. Wine, cheese, dried fruits, nuts, gifts. A big complex with a Casa de Hamburger, a Casa de Coffee, etc., etc.

I asked an employe: "Where's your Casa de Bathroom?"

We drove up here to take a peek at the University of California at Santa Cruz where we are sending a couple of offspring later this month.

It's a beautiful campus. Six, and eventually eight, separate colleges, set in the high woods above the city. You hike from class to class on wooded trails (or you can ride a horse).

A young, long-haired drama teacher showed us around the dorm rooms which you can decorate any way you want as long as it is within fire regulations. A student lounge, decorated and furnished by students, a greenhouse—another student project.

It's an independent study school. The teacher said: "We believe in the students running their own lives up here. There are almost no hard and fast rules."

Not many dissident students. If you are going to be dissatis-fied, you'll have to be dissatisfied with yourself.

He said: "About the only thing that ever bugs anybody up here is the constant clatter of people around all the time. When that happens the best thing to do is go and sit in the meadow over there and listen to the silence."

From the meadow there is a view over the tops of trees and far out into the blue Pacific.

We are ready to come home, now. To drive out of the fog seascapes and down through the sunbaked flatlands of central California. (Saroyan country, though he might get lost, too, among the "Terrible Herbst" gas stations and the "Okie Frijole" cafes.)

I used to live in this country and seemed comfortable. But the cool breezes coming off Mission Bay have soaked into and thinned my blood these past seven years.

Now, unless I am wrapped from head to toe in air condition-ing, the heat of the Big Valley turns me to ashes in hours.

At Bakersfield—one of California's most aptly named cities—we will turn east and climb the Tehachapis then drive down into the high desert, part of the Mojave.

We will jockey for road position there with huge produce trucks carrying cargos to and from markets and every kind of camper vehicle you can imagine coming down from the Sierra.

It's a little bit longer route but we will not go through the Los Angeles traffic headache at the tailend of the Labor Day weekend.

And that's called planning ahead. (A little lesson we learned from independent study.)

If I Ever Come Back

Up early in the blue morning, massaged into life with rich, black Cafe Incasa, the coffee from Guatemala.

I use the instant. (On the label it says "Instantaneo!" The label is enough to wake you up.)

The children groaned in the sack. I said: "All right, hop to it! I know you're awake."

If it wasn't a school day, they'd be up at 7 a.m. watching the cartoons.

I said: "Now! Instantaneo!"

The only ones who get up early without complaint are the cats. They are in the kitchen, helping me make my coffee, shining my pants leg with their backs.

They are purring: "Man, we *love* you. Man, we are *starving.*"

These cats are all sugary affection before breakfast. But, as soon as they are fed, they cool down and go sit in the sun.

Recently science made a little study on reincarnation. "If you could come back as any animal, which animal would you choose?"

Females for the most part chose cats.

Science never asks me anything. (Though I have asked science *plenty* of things over the years.) *If* science asked me what I would like to come back as, I certainly would not pick a cat.

Actually, I would tell science I do not intend to come back, because I do not intend to go.

However, if I had no choice, I would choose something more exotic than a lamebrained house cat.

Something like a Tasmanian Devil or maybe a three-toed sloth, which is very big in the crosswords.

Or I might come back as a grasshopper. Spend my days hippity-hop in the barley fields. (I'm pretty good at that.)

A gorilla. If I came back as a big, black, hairy gorilla, I'll bet I'd have no trouble prying sluggish children out of bed for school.

I once had a Great-uncle George who swore his cat was the reincarnation of his fourth wife, Martha.

"She acts just like Martha," he said. "Eats and sleeps all day. Wants in when you put her out. Wants out when you put her in.

Besides, she has this certain fishy look in her eye. That's Martha all right."

"Stuff and nonsense," said his fifth wife, Jane. "That's old man talk."

But Aunt Jane shooed that cat out of their room every time she tried to go in. (We kids thought it was really creepy. "Gee, do you think that *could* be Aunt Martha?")

School Days, School Days

Everybody went back to school in murderous 92 degrees. (That's the killing temperature, police report.)

First reports on new teachers, new assignments are coming in. Some of them are killing.

One child—I don't dare come closer than that in identification—got the P.E. teacher that "looks like a chicken."

Another still doesn't know what his classes are. "We just stood around for three hours in the heat. Man, it was *all* messed up."

The nursery school muffin started kindergarten this year. She is on a split shift. Spends the morning at nursery schol, the afternoon at kindergarten.

I took a little poll while driving her home, and found she gives the nursery school the edge. "There's more things to do at nursery school," she said.

(This evaluation is based on total number of swings, slides, dolls, types of crayons, different colors of clay, etc., etc.)

In the days when I was clicking picket fences, we had nicknames for all the teachers. Outside their presence, they were called "The Hawk" or "The Bulldog" or "Curly Bill."

This was at Christian Brothers in Sacramento. A combination of upper grades and high school. (Yes, it's the order that makes the wine. We know all about that. A lot of it was stored in secret basement rooms that were not all that secret.)

"Curly Bill" was Brother William, the principal. The nickname wasn't malicious. He simply had a mass of curly brown hair.

"The Hawk" was Brother Vincent. What eyes he had! He

could spot cigarette smoke the full length of the football field on a foggy day.

(He was fooled for awhile when somebody invented the "smoke sandwich." A lighted cigarette between two slices of bread.)

"The Bulldog"—I forget his name—looked just like that. Short, pug-faced, and shoulders as thick as trees. Somebody said he had been a marine sergeant.

It was a small school—only 500 boys from sixth through 12th grade—but it was tough. It had to be, stuck between the city's two big ones, Sacramento and McClatchy.

We played the big ones eye to eye on the football field. Sometimes we won the game. We almost always won the fight afterwards.

We *had* to play the big schools. The other small Catholic schools around the area, like St. Mary's of Stockton, had barred us from competition. (They accused us of playing like lions instead of Christians.)

Those days are gone. The school is even gone. Now, boys and girls go to high school *together* in Sacramento. (An idea that would have horrified us back in the 1940s.)

Dear old Golden Rule days.

The Business of Making Jerky

Jerky was the western man's answer to tough meat and the lack of refrigeration. It is simply meat which has been sliced into thin strips and cured by drying.

It will last a long time—even when you're eating it.

On the frontier, jerky was the mainstay of Indians, pioneers and cowboys. It is now used as an easy-to-pack energy food by campers, hunters and back-packers.

And college students wash it down with beer.

In the days of the early west, it took several days of drying the meat in the sun or over a green wood fire to make jerky.

However, a few years ago an old Indian sold me the old Indian trick of making jerky overnight in a modern gas or electric oven. He charged me $2 for the secret, which he swore he translated from drawings made by the ancestors of his tribe in a hidden cave in Utah.

I have no reason to doubt him but, true or not, the recipe has been well worth the $2 investment to me. It does produce jerky which, if not instant, can be made overnight. And it's a lot better for children's teeth than junk.

Also, it comes in handy when a child comes up to you and announces, "There's nothing to do." Just slip the kid a piece of jerky and it will keep him busy for quite awhile.

So, I am passing this secret on to my readers, with apologies for those who wasted postage to get a copy mailed to them. And never mind the $2.

Cut your beef (or venison, or whatever) into thin strips—about one-fourth inch at most. This is easiest if the meat has been frozen and is partially thawed.

Place the strips in a glass cake pan. (The glass cake pan made me a little suspicious of the old Indian.) Using a basting brush, garnish them with liquid smoke, which is available in any grocery store.

Use the liquid smoke sparingly, but make sure each piece gets some. It's the most important ingredient.

After garnishing one layer of strips, season them with seasoning salt. Then sprinkle just the slightest bit of sugar on top. Pepper and regular salt may be added. (You can experiment with those after your first batch—but don't forget the seasoning salt and liquid smoke.) After one layer of strips has been completed, put another layer on top and repeat the process. Place the next layer of strips crosswise. The pan should have three or four layers in it.

Next, let the pan sit and soak up these seasonings for at least four hours.

After that, place the strips on an oven rack—not in a pan and not touching each other—and put them in the oven.

Leave them overnight, 8 to 12 hours, in the oven at a temperature of 150 degrees. On a gas oven, the pilot light will usually furnish this much heat. On an electric oven, if the temperature range starts at 200, set it at that and leave the door slightly open.

You will have to experiment somewhat on the amount of time you leave your jerky in the oven. It depends on how you like your jerky. Eight hours will give you a different consistency than 12—and the thickness of the meat strips also will have something to do with how long you leave it in the oven.

The next morning, you can remove the jerky and eat it, or store it in a glass jar.

Put some in your child's school lunch, and it will stretch out his lunch hour to all afternoon.

PART FOUR

After finishing this final part, I expected the publisher to throw some kind of little shindig for me. I distinctly remember reading something in my contract about "the party of the last part."

I'll probably get an invitation any day now.

Haole in Hawaii

Waikiki Beach is wall-to-wall high rise now, and the sidewalks of Kalakaua Avenue are bumper-to-bumper people. Most of them American Legionnaires. "The biggest convention in the island's history," said one paper.

We (and the Legionnaires) come from all over the mainland. From California, Ohio, New York, New Jersey, Alabama. All a little cockeyed from the time change.

But all barefoot in paradise.

We came in on United's big-bellied 747 from Los Angeles. A quick five-hour flight. Just enough time for a cocktail party, dinner and a movie.

And then, Aloha, everybody. "If you will look out the windows to the left . . ."

The airlines saturate you with Hawaii from the time you step on the plane. The stewardesses, dressed in flowered gowns, hand you a glass of pineapple juice and island music fills the cabin. (Hardly seems right to call the inside of a 747 a "cabin." It's bigger than the city room.)

They used to wait until they had reached the halfway point before changing from uniforms to island garb and turning on the music.

But no more. Now the movie is playing during the halfway point. And I expect the stewardesses are counting up the $2 fees it costs to rent a headset.

Still, it's all part of the bite. You don't get to paradise on your good looks, angel.

We caught a few waves on an outrigger canoe—$1 a wave—before lunch. The more you look like you can paddle, the closer the beach boy puts you to the front. (I drew No. 2 paddle. Thank you.)

I wore my trousers. I had seen other people wearing clothing on outrigger rides.

What I *hadn't* seen was that those other people came in from the ride soaking wet.

Also, nobody told me that the closer you sit toward the front, the more water you get in the face. (And on the trousers.) You act as sort of a shield for the people behind you.

This haole (newcomer) nearly drowned. But he is learning fast, brudda.

In the canoe, going out and coming in, the beach boy shouts instructions in fluent English and Japanese. (More than 250,000 Japanese tourists here this year.)

"Everybody change sides. *Now,* paddle Fast! *Faster!*" Then "Ichiban something-or-other . . ."

But back on the beach, with the other beach boys, he reverts to pidgin English.

It's a chop suey shortcut to the language.

"Hey brudda, whassamatah, you da kine wear pants on outrigger?"

I told him I just wanted to rinse them out with a little salt water. (Also rinsed out my checkbook, lighter, hotel key, few small bills, and a small notebook.)

Then back to the hotel for lunch and a short nap.

I would have gotten enough sleep last night, but I could hear the music and chatter from a half-dozen nightclubs below our hotel.

The nightclubs on Waikiki close at 4 a.m.

Waikiki is in Honolulu on the island of Oahu. (The address is Honolulu, Hawaii, but it is not on the island of Hawaii, as a lot of mainlanders think.)

Oahu is The Capital Island. Only the third largest of the seven, but with four-fifths of the citizens and more than 80 percent of the tourists.

King Kamehameha added Oahu to his all-island kingdom when he and his warriors from Hawaii landed at Maunalua Bay and pushed the Oahu men all the way to the edge of Nuuanu Pali.

Then they forced them to jump off the cliffs to their death.

That was in 1795. The king and his men sprawled out on Waikiki Beach and had peace and quiet for 25 golden years. Then the missionaries came, and the rest followed.

Waikiki is a big part of blue Hawaii, and the tradewinds blow as warm as mother love there the same as on the other outer islands. But it wasn't what we were looking for.

One night and half-a-day were fine. Then we collected our bags and took the $6 cab ride to the airport.

There a bright-colored little 737 of the Aloha Airlines waited to carry us in 27 minutes to lush Kauai, The Garden Island.

Golden beaches, misty Waialeale (the ancient volcano), and something green blooming almost everywhere.

The land of the Menehunes, Hawaii's legendary elves.

Maybe I will interview one.

One minute sunshine, one minute soft rain at the end of the island of Kauai. It doesn't bother anybody but the people trying to take pictures.

("Okay, everybody, look out toward the surf. No, wait, dammit. The light changed again. Lemme get another reading.")

But nobody gets up from the beach. The volleyball game doesn't stop. It's baby-kiss rain. Just nice.

We are at Hanalei Colony, almost the end of the road— Hawaii 56. Whoever built this little cluster of condominiums had me in mind. No phones. No TV. Only a few people.

If I had a baseball, I could throw it from my lanai into the warm surf. I could also throw it into the Anchorage Bar, but I might knock over a very excellent mai tai.

No swimming pool. No clock on the wall. And I could reach out my bedroom window and pick a ripe papaya for breakfast.

Yesterday, thank goodness, my watch stem broke. Today we don't know what time it is in paradise. (But you don't see me crying about that.)

Pele, the fire goddess, used to live here. But no more. She was in love with King Lohiau but Kauai was too wet for her.

She tried several times to dig a dry pit where she could start her fire. But the rain kept tumbling down. (Mt. Waialeale here is the wettest place on earth.)

Finally Pele hung it all up and moved over to the big island— Hawaii.

But they say she comes back to visit now and then.

If you see a little white dog trotting down the road, or an old, old woman—well, that *could* be Pele.

The road ends about four miles from here at Ke's Beach. (Just call it the End Beach.) Go up the trail from there and you'll find those former hippies who finally got to heaven.

They live in makeshift camps in the Ironwood Forest.

Beautiful young dropouts from the world. Tanned young mothers with their babies riding on one hip. And their golden long-haired men.

All living off the fruit of the land, the fish of the sea, and the occasional check from home (or the government).

Each midday they come out of the woods and line the road, hitchhiking to Mrs. Chin Young's.

Mrs. Chin Young's is a general merchandise store, a few miles down to the little town of Hanalei.

It's a big wooden building with three doors. First door, post office—where the checks arrive. Second door, Bank of Hawaii—where the checks are cashed. Third door, store— where the checks are spent.

Those who get checks on a regular enough basis sometimes can get a charge account at Mrs. Chin Young's.

She has two separate checkout stands. One for cash, one for charge.

It cuts down confusion.

Yesterday we picked up fresh pineapple for breakfast at Mrs. Chin Young's.

"One pineapple. Dat 13 cents."

"How tings on de mainland, brudda?"

Yesterday we also drove over the Hanalei Plantation. It was Emile de Becques' (Rossano Brazzi) home in the movie "South Pacific."

Today it is a big resort and getting bigger. The planning commission last week okayed construction of 64 more dwelling units and another restaurant-bar at the plantation.

All to be built on slopes of 50 to 80 percent.

On the way home, we stopped at Lumahai Beach, the nurses' beach in "South Pacific." Where Mitzi Gaynor washed that man right out of her hair.

The Hawaii Visitors Bureau says it is the most photographed beach in all the islands. (Maybe so. I took at least six shots of it.)

Somewhere in between the plantation and the beach, we found a beautiful little waterfall.

I told my wife: "Go stand under it, honey, and I'll take your picture."

She said: "Okay."

So we hiked up the little trail and down the little trail, and finally reached the little pond. She stepped into it, and the waterfall trickled down behind her.

I said: "You know, to really make it authentic looking, like in the postcards, you ought to take off your . . . err . . ."

She said: *"John!"*

We packed a pineapple, a papaya and a six-pack of Primo beer and climbed into our little U-drive car for a leisurely tour of The Garden Island of Hawaii.

First stop: Waipahee Slippery Slide, built on whatever day of creation God decided to take a break and make toys.

The Waipahee Slippery Slide is just that, a slide of about 25 steep feet down a smooth rock stream into a deep blue pool.

To reach the slide, you have to ask questions. There are no signs on Highway 56. And, though it is on all six maps we have, there are no detailed instructions.

Anyway, stop in the little town of Anahola on Anahola Bay and ask somebody. (If the little store by the post office is open, there is a rough, handmade map on its wall.)

A short distance from Anahola (toward Lihue) you take a cutoff road which leads you about five miles up the mountains through the sugar cane fields. Then another cutoff (this one *does* have a sign) on a pretty bad dirt road which you follow to the end. Maybe four miles.

Then you get out and walk. But what a walk! A third of a mile on a narrow, winding trail through ferns, white orchids, wild gardenias and blazing red hibiscus.

(Pick a flower for your girl's hair. Give her a kiss. Aloha!)

Finally you reach the pool. And it is full of kids. The haole kids slide down the rock with mock screams or giggle fits. The Hawaiian kids slide too, but they also jump or dive right off the edge of the cliff. It's scary because that's a pretty small target down there.

"Hey, Kimo, come down slide."

"No mon. Jump mo' better."

The adults take pictures.

We came out of the forest and drove on down through Lihue (the island's biggest town) to Poipu Beach to listen to the dragon.

At the end of Poipu Beach there is a hole in the bed of lava rock on the sea edge called "The Spouting Horn."

The surf beats fiercely at rocks and every few seconds a giant stream of white water spouts out of the hole.

Between spouts there is this snorting, breathing noise under the rocks. The early Hawaiian natives believed it was a dragon trapped under the rocks.

As the sun began to settle comfortably in the Pacific, we stopped at the big shopping center in Lihue to slip into some fresh clothes. (Not *in* the shopping center. They happen to have a couple of big dressing rooms. One called "Kanes" and one called "Wahines.")

I said: "Now we will move on down the road where, for the price of something tall and cool, we will watch the torchlighting ceremony at the Coco Palms. And I picked a hibiscus from a nearby tree and pinned it in my blonde wahine's hair.

The last of the big-time spenders.

As we reached the grove, the home of Hawaiian royalty in ancient days, the coco palms were black cardboard cutouts against the twilight sky.

We had barely sipped on a couple of fruity mai tais before the torchbearers appeared on the small bridge over the resort lagoon.

One bearer faced toward the sea and blew a single lonesome note from the conch shell. Then toward the valley. Then toward the mountain.

After the shell is sounded and the drum is pounded, the runners streak through the grove, lighting up the torches so the whole area looks like a Christmas tree.

With all the flames flickering and the smoke (kerosene, I think) pouring out, I suppose they would call such a thing pollution on the mainland.

But here, where the trade winds air-condition all seven islands day and night, they call it Beautiful Hawaii.

"I am go-inng to the island of the valeeee." My wife has been singing that line for weeks. Now we are finally here. Maui is the Island of the Valley.

We caught Hawaiian's afternoon nonstop bird in Kauai and 37 minutes over blue water put us in mystic old Maui.

There are a lot of spooky legends in Maui. And I am superstitious enough to believe them all.

(If you see a spirit beckoning to you at Kaiwaloa Heiau, don't follow it, man. You'll never return.)

We picked up a rental car at the airport and drove over to Lahaina, the first capital of the Hawaiian Kingdom and once the rowdy whaling port of the world for more than 40 years.

It was a wild, wild town. The whalers would pull into port after months at sea and proceed to raise old bill-o. They weren't in town to look for souvenirs.

Finally it got so bad that King Kamehameha had to build a special prison to house any sailor who was not back on his ship by sundown.

Today all the lusty taverns of old have been turned into gift and curio shops. Even The Whale's Tail, which still had its battle scars of countless brawls only a few years ago, is a place to buy Hawaiian shirts and muumuus today.

And you can hardly see the wharf for the tour buses parked in front of it.

Where have all the flower children gone? You can find a lot of them in Lahaina.

Living in paradise on small change.

Maui is like two islands. Two high volcanic areas connected by a low, rich valley of mostly cane fields. "Pure cane sugar, from Hawaii," as the commercial goes.

A lot of politicians are trying to get Hawaii to diversify its agriculture. To cut island food prices. "If we can grow cane, pineapple and papaya, we can grow other stuff too," one of them said.

One grower gave it a try. He planted 600 acres in potatoes and cornered the market. He now supplies more than 60 percent of the potatoes for all the islands.

A lot of resorts are growing in west Maui, from Lahaina all along the Kaanapali Coast. Big high-rise resorts.

I predict Kaanapali will be the next Waikiki Beach of the islands.

We drove almost to the end of Highway 30, to a little place tucked neatly into Napili Bay. Napili Surf Beach. A stretch of golden sand caressed by trade winds and warm, clear water.

Where the mongooses and the mynah birds play.

A lady at the hotel told me: "They imported the mongooses here some years ago to get rid of the mice.

"The trouble was, although the mongoose will eat rodents, they are day animals. The mice on this island are nocturnal. They come out at night.

"So now there are mongoose *and* mice."

(You can look that up if you want. It is not "mongeese.")

Napili Surf Beach does not have a beach good for surfing. In fact, there's hardly any surf at all. The waves just sort of lap the shoreline.

But it's a marvelous beach for just snorkeling around. All kinds of different colored tropical fish to see. Several reefs to stand on if you need a rest.

(I stood on one quite awhile. Being sorely in need of rest.)

This is haole country now. You would have a hard time finding a Hawaiian on the west end of Maui. Unless you go to a floor show.

And it has all calmed down from the old days.

When the missionaries came to Maui, they said: "God is in your hearts and everywhere." But the whaling men said: "No God west of the Horn."

Well, God finally came to Maui. And so did Sheraton, and Royal, and etcetera, etc., etc.

October Ghosts

Smoky blue evenings of October. "On Indian summer nights, the corn shocks turn into tepees and the ghosts of long gone Indians dance silently in the haze."

That's the old bedtime storyteller at work. I like to throw a spooky touch in my stories.

It makes my listeners *anxious* to go to bed. (Covers over the head.)

"You're going to give them nightmares," said their mother.

I said: "They love them creepy. The creepier the better. I read somewhere it's good for them."

Actually, the youngest boy found the article. Some psychologist explained that horror movies and TV fright shows release some kind of healthy waves in children's brains.

"See," he said, "it's good for me to watch scary shows."

The idea seemed to boil down to letting the child live out his violent tendencies on the screen. By watching somebody else take the ax to a victim, the child would be less inclined to pick up an ax himself.

I think that's an excellent idea. (However, I still keep the hatchet hidden.)

When I was a child, I *loved* horror movies. The more horrible, the better.

I have a total recall of the first movie I ever went to by myself. My mother dropped me off at a downtown theater in Phoenix, and gave me 10-cents to go see "Snow White."

I walked up to the boxoffice and asked them if they had the time. And my mother's car pulled away and turned the corner.

Then I walked across the street, to another theater, and put my dime down for "Son of Frankenstein."

Wow! I nearly died of delicious fright. That night I had some absolutely beautiful nightmares.

I said: "Once upon a time, in a dark old mansion near Dead Man's Lake, there lived a man named Conrad. He was a widower, because his beautiful wife, Coleen, had drowned in the lake seven years before.

One night, from the lake, he heard this strange, wailing voice calling—"Connnn-raaaad. Connnn-raaaad."

"Aiiieee," the children cried, diving for the covers.

She said: "Now *stop* it! Good heavens, I'd have nightmares if I listened to a story like that."

I said: "Why do you keep interrupting? How do you know, maybe that's just the Avon lady rowing across the lake."

She said: "I know who is going to have to be up with them all night if they can't sleep because of bad dreams."

I said: "Okay, to continue. The voice yelling 'Connnn-raaaad' was indeed the Avon lady, rowing across the lake to deliver some after shave and a jeweled lipstick Conrad planned to give his mother for Christmas. And everybody lived happily ever after. Now, go to sleep."

The kids said: "Gee, that's no good of a story. Gee."

Midnight Lady on a Fence

Misty evenings around the old castle. The chilling fog comes swirling in from the sea and gives a ghostly look to the hillside lights around us.

Last night there was a lady in a nightgown standing on our fence.

This was about midnight, and the breeze moved her gown and blonde hair. And I imagine if any of the neighbors saw this spooky sight, they probably crossed themselves and put their heads under the covers.

For ladies in nightgowns on fences at midnight are not all that common a sight in Seaside Suburbia. And I do not recommend them for weak hearts.

This particular lady was standing on the fence, calling a name over and over again.

She was calling: "Here kitty, kitty, kitty."

I should say here that this is not eyewitness reporting, for I was sound asleep when it all happened. However, the lady herself told me about it, when she came back to bed.

It seems we had a cat on a cold tin roof.

(See, children, there is a reasonable explanation for everything. Next time you see a lady in a nightgown on a fence at midnight, why, think nothing of it.)

She said: "I kept hearing it crying, I had to get up and do something."

It seems this particular cat can go *up* a tree full speed. But it is not equipped with a reverse gear. It cannot come down.

It goes up the small tree, hangs a left at metal awning over the

second-story windows and parks there for the night with its horn stuck.

I said: "If you're going to go out at midnight and stand on the fence in your nightgown, at least take a gun with you."

A midnight lady on a fence might prove intriguing to somebody. But a midnight lady on a fence with a gun in her hand—well, I can't imagine *anybody* who would come close to a sight like that.

It all made for lively chatter around the breakfast table.

"Did you really go out and stand on the fence, mom?"

She said: "I had to do something. I thought I could reach it from the fence top."

They said: "In your nightgown?"

She said: "It's a very modest nightgown. I couldn't find my robe."

They said: "Gee, mom, you're weird."

She actually did not rescue the cat herself. She had to wake one of the boys to climb up on the roof and get it.

She said: "I knew *you* wouldn't climb on top of the house at midnight."

That is correct.

She said: "I suppose you're probably going to put something about this in the paper."

I said: "Why should I? Doesn't everybody have a wife who walks fences at midnight in her nightgown?"

(Wow! This is even *better* than sleepwalking!)

Grandma's Terrible Threats

"I'll whop you so hard it'll make your shirttail pop up your back like a window curtain!" That was Grandma Mitchell speaking to her grandchildren back in the 1930s.

She was a puny little woman of something less than 90 pounds. Other memories of her are vague. There was the gray hair in a tight bun. And, as I recall, her only sin was snuff.

But she was full of dire threats that, if taken seriously, would freeze the blood of an Apache. We loved them.

"If you don't get that wood chopped right now you're gonna wake up sleeping in a marble orchard!"

I know that sometimes we would press her patience on purpose just to hear what marvelous new threat would roll off her tongue.

Sometimes she would repeat herself in her threats, but she had an extensive repertoire and, by the time she got around to reruns, they seemed fresh again.

It was a kind of early-day literature.

Hardly a week went by in my childhood when I was not threatened with skinning. "If you don't get out of those cookies I'm going to skin you alive."

Once, I boldly asked: "Grandma, what are you going to do with the skin?"

It was a mistake. And I nearly got skinned alive for it.

Among the more common misfortunes that hung over my head at various times were the possibilities of being beaten to within an inch of my life, and getting my head pinched off.

Then there were the classics.

"Child, I'm going to kick that backside of yours so hard you'll have to open your mouth to shine your shoes."

We thought and thought about that one, and never did exactly figure it out. But it was a wonderful threat. One of grandma's best.

It was the kind of threat you could brag about at school.

It was nothing to be threatened with punishments which would make my ears ring, my eyeteeth rattle, or my toes curl.

But it was a special occasion when grandma would say: "I'm going to reach down your throat, grab your toenails, and *pull*!"

You don't find this kind of child discipline touted much in the magazines these days. But we kind of enjoyed it. The threats were so absolutely ridiculous that we loved them.

Grandma has been sleeping in a green field in the hills of the Ozarks for many, many years now. We carried her frail body back there on a train when I was still only 10 years old.

And we still miss her.

(And if she were alive, and knew I printed all this about her, she'd probably "snatch me baldheaded.")

Picnic in the Rain

Chilly fall evenings, but it's warm and cozy inside. I put a thick green pepper tree log on the fireplace and turned on the gas jet. Instant cheer!

The cats spread out on the hearth and purred in time to the dance of the flames.

The first rains of winter came over the weekend. Lightning and thunder in the black sky. The children said: "There goes our Sunday picnic."

I said: "Nonsense. We'll still go."

About 11 a.m. Sunday we were in the supermarket, buying charcoal, hamburger, cold beer, pickles, and potato chips.

Outside the rain was pounding down. (And the checkout clerk looked at us as if we had rain on the brain.)

"I promised a picnic, and that's what we'll have," I told the children. I started up the engine and the windshield wipers.

We drove north on Highway 5, then turned off on Via De La Valle. Winding through the golf courses and estates of beautiful Rancho Santa Fe. Then a turnoff to Felicita Park.

The sun was shining bright in the park. The tables, newly painted and scrubbed by the night rain, glistened. And there was not another soul around.

Everybody was pretty impressed. I said: "It's nothing. Just an old Eskimo trick. Just head into the wind of a storm and pretty soon you'll find sunshine."

We started up the charcoal, turned on the World Series, and stretched out on the sweet smelling grass.

The children headed for the playground.

The wife said: "When did you ever know an old Eskimo?"

I said: "I never did. But that's what I would do if I were an old Eskimo."

The park was like a pretty package, wrapped with a rainbow in the western sky.

The hot dogs, hamburgers, and barbecue beans got done at just about the exact time that the black clouds moved in and filled up the blue sky overhead.

The children came running from the merry-go-round. "It's going to rain! It's going to rain!"

I said: "Don't panic, Chicken Little. Go get a plate and eat."

It was a race to see which got down first, the beans or the rain. However, we made the meal, and ran to the car, carrying baskets, paper bags and blankets.

The sunshine lasted just a little more than an hour. It was a short picnic, but a good one.

"What will we do now?" asked the children.

I said: "Don't worry. I know a couple of excellent wine tasting rooms in Escondido, where it is not raining inside. Then I know where there are a few more logs to throw on our fireplace, and where some popcorn might be obtained."

I am full of old Eskimo tricks.

Roaming the Gold Country

We have been cruising on a 35-foot bus through California's gold rush country, blessed right now with the golden colors of autumn and air as fresh as a milkmaid's smile.

We had morning coffee in Hornitos, a withered little map dot that once was among the noisiest and most violent towns of the old West.

Bandit Joaquin Murietta's secret escape tunnel is supposed to be under the tree-shaded plaza, and Cherokee Bill, horse thief, is buried in the little "riff-raff cemetery" on the hill.

Built by Mexicans who had been run out of Quartzburg and nourished by the rich veins of gold nearby, Honitos grew to a population of 15,000 in a few years, and saloons and dance-halls lined the streets.

Eventually, though, the day came when Wells Fargo was no longer shipping out $40,000 a day in ore. When gold went, so did the people.

Today the population is less than 150. Hornitos lives quietly with its colorful ghosts.

The sign you see entering town reads: "This place is like heaven to us. Don't drive like hell through it."

Out of Hornitos and on up the hill to Mariposa, a key gateway to Yosemite Park, Bret Harte country.

We are touring with 40 members of the San Diego Historical Society. To see as much as possible in five days, tour director Mack Sugg makes short stops. It's necessary. You could spend as much as an afternoon in any of 100 historic places.

I wanted to see the offices of the Mariposa Gazette, the oldest California newspaper in continuous publication. But we stopped only for 15 minutes to view the old courthouse.

(I didn't even see that. I had to run to the drug store for aspirin and a stomach settler. We history buffs had lifted a few to Murietta the night before.)

From Mariposa, it's a spectacular drive (I wouldn't use that word, but Sunset magazine has coined that stretch "the spectacular highway") down the pine-studded grade and into Tuolumne—say it "Two-wah-lum-nee"—County.

Lunch in Sonora, the county seat. I used to live and work in this town. It looks like a typical little backwoods town, where not much influence from the big city is ever felt.

However, one of the three leading industries up there is motion pictures. If you've ever seen the movies "High Noon" or "For Whom the Bell Tolls" or any western series on television, you've seen some of this country.

Over to Columbia, the gem of the Mother Lode, after lunch. Columbia, the entire city, is a living historic state park, completely restored to look as it did in the days of the 49ers. (Here's where Gary Cooper walked down the street to face four gunmen, and Grace Kelly copped out on him.)

Columbia was one of the richest diggings in the West. It once teemed with more than 20,000 people and came within two votes of becoming the state capital.

Today it is shaded by huge oaks and crowded with milling tourists. Unless somebody puts a dime in the nickelodeon at the Douglas bar, about the only noise you hear is the constant clicking of cameras.

Columbia is, in spirit, what San Diego's Old Town will one day be—a living, working historic state park. The only difference will be the eras they depict. Columbia's is 1849. Old Town's historic era has not yet been pinned down to the exact years.

However, one day the traffic will stop in Old Town, the shop people will be required to wear costumes of the period, and the place will become a live memorial to our heritage.

(The state must be careful what year it picks. At one time, the soldiers were going around in armor and the Indians were going around in Indian skins.)

Tomorrow's report will come to you from the bridal suite in Nevada City's ancient National Hotel.

It is golden autumn in the Mother Lode now. A rainbow trout rises slowly to the stream's surface. A rifle's crack shatters the earth morning stillness.

The day begins.

You can fly into the Columbia airport, providing you arrive in a small enough plane. The runway won't handle the jet jobs, or even the big prop planes.

Clearance to land from the tower means there are no deer on the runway—right at this moment. But keep a close eye.

Columbia, itself, is a town which was born in the Gold Rush, and almost played out when the mines did. Now it has been restored to an 1849 look, and exists as a living, inhabited historical state park.

But Columbia had its day. By 1853 it was the second largest city in California. Only San Francisco was bigger.

And you can still hear the story from residents up here that,

"Columbia lost out on being the capital of California by only two votes."

Not exactly true.

Columbia unwittingly gave up its chance to become the state capital to save old Pete Nichols from the gallows.

The then thriving town was being promoted throughout the West by a new and active Columbia Boosters Club. The state capital, at that time, was temporarily situated in Benicia, in the east San Francisco Bay area.

But the Columbia boosters had been circulating a petition for some months, and now had more than 10,000 signatures from local citizens requesting the capital be moved to their town.

About this time, Pete Nichols, of nearby Saw Mill Flat, and John Perioit of Pine Log, got into a fight in a Columbia saloon over the attentions of one of the barmaids.

Peroit ended up on the tavern floor dead, with Nichols' knife in him.

A resourceful young attorney named Horace Bull was appointed counsel for Nichols but despite his efforts, Nichols was found guilty by a jury six days later and sentenced to hang.

The execution date was set for 10 days after the trial.

Then Horace Bull went into action.

Bull went to the Boosters Club and informed them he was going to Benecia to file an appeal for his client and would be glad to do the club the favor of dropping off its petition on the governor's desk.

This seemed like a practical idea to the club, so they handed the petition over to Bull.

The attorney then proceeded to cut the portion of the petition containing the signatures off, and pasted it at the bottom of a request to Governor John Bigler to pardon his client, Pete Nichols.

When Governor Bigler saw the request signed by 10,000 voters, he immediately commuted Nichols' sentence.

Nichols naturally disappeared as soon as he was released from jail. And Columbia lost it's chance to become the capital of California.

The attorney made it up to the town, when they found out about his trick, by offering to give Columbia a new fire engine.

The town shrugged its shoulders and accepted.

(The fire engine was stolen from the docks of San Francisco and delivered to Columbia. But that's another story.)

There is a brief, polite and personal note on one wall of the old museum in San Andreas—a few short words from one friend to another:

". . . hoping this letter finds you well and in good health. Me and Charlie is sentenced to hang at 5 o'clock tomorrow for robbery. Goodbye, and give regards to Joe, Church and Bob. Sincerely, John."

It's a tiny fragment of the rip-roaring history of this Mother Lode country during the days of the Gold Rush.

Hanging for robbery seems harsh today. But in those mid-1800s, if you took a man's shovel, pack, or horse, you took his means of staying alive.

There's also humor, albeit the gallows type, in the justice of the "diggings." Placerville's famous dinner dish, "Hangtown Fry," was invented by a condemned man.

Asked what he wanted for his final meal, the man cleverly asked for "Oysters wrapped with eggs and bacon."

The last meal was an ironclad privilege. And the man gained a week's time with his request.

It took that long to get oysters from San Francisco.

Crisp, clear days in the Mother Lode mountains. The air could sell for $2 a breath in Los Angeles.

There's a little smoke. But it's hard to think of it as pollution. It drifts in from the little lumber mills, carrying the fragrances of cedar, fir, and sugar-pine.

We have been looking at this country at a rapid clip. There's a lot of it to cover in five days—figuring it took a day to get up here and will take another to get home.

We make a lot of picture stops. Tour director Mack Sugg says: "Now, we'll just stop at this monument for anybody who wants a picture. The rest please stay in the bus."

Well, everybody wants a picture of *everything*. (I swear, if he stopped at a fireplug, at least five people would pile out and take a picture of it.)

I am putting these notes together in the bridal suite of the old National Hotel in Nevada City. It's a Victorian gothic building, the oldest hotel in continuous operation in the state.

Some of the biggest of the state's mining deals were made in the hardwood bar that was brought up here, piece by piece, from the John Spreckels home on San Francisco's Nob Hill.

What are we doing in the bridal suite?

Well, the bridegroom is slaving over a cold typewriter, while the bride is giving tours.

"Just look at those chairs. Why, the lamps alone must be worth a fortune. And those drawers, all the way up to the ceiling!"

Somebody said: "Oh, are you writing? What are you writing about?"

I said: "About some people who got hanged for almost nothing."

She said: "Well, don't let us bother you. My, have you ever seen such a beautiful canopy bed?"

(There's also a beautiful antique color television set in here. Maybe I can catch an antique movie on it later on.)

Witch Behind the Dishwasher

Halloween has already arrived in this household. I saw my first witch lurking behind the portable dishwasher last night.

"BOO!" she said, and then went into a pretty hideous cackle for a 5-year-old witch. "Hah, hah, hah. Did I scare you?"

"Did you scare me?" I said. "Good heavens, I think you have given me four new gray hairs, and possibly turned my liver white. Go ask your mother for the smelling salts."

Well, this admission was greeted with a good deal of glee and happiness.

There is no better news for a fledgling witch, freshly outfitted in mask and cape from the dime store, than to hear she is causing successful heart attacks.

"I scared Rover, too," she said. "He ran under the bed."

"I'm not surprised," I said. (Rover is the cat with the name of a dog and the nerves of a chicken.)

"Next year I am going to be a fairy," she said. "And the next year I am going to be a ghost."

"Those are a couple of reasonable ambitions," I said. "I think I might be able to cope better with a fairy behind the dishwasher. I'll think about the ghost when the time comes."

She said: "And the next year I am going to be a bride, and the next year I am going to be a princess, and the next year . . ."

I said: "My goodness, you've got your Halloween career pretty well mapped out right up to middleage, haven't you?"

She said: "What are you going to be?"

I said: "I am thinking seriously of being Sleeping Beauty. In fact, I am going in right now to the living room couch and practice. Please don't let anyone kiss me awake for at least thirty minutes."

Halloween is probably my favorite holiday, and I have researched the subject until I know all the proper ways to celebrate it, and then some.

I know that if you plait a pitchfork with a little straw and wave it in the air, you are likely to singe a witch's broom as she passes by.

I know a Halloween bonfire will get rid of demons and spirits.

I am aware that if a single young lady eats a Halloween apple in front of a mirror, the face of her future husband will appear.

And I am fully prepared to spend Halloween evening bribing

small boys not to wax my car windows by plying them with Tootsie Rolls and Sugar Pops.

And I'm also ready for a friend of mine who drops by every Halloween at about 11 p.m. with a martini glass in his hand and a silly grin on his face.

"Trick or treat," he will say, and I will ask him in. It is somewhat of a Halloween ritual with us.

It also seems to get rid of a certain amount of evil spirits.

The 5 a.m. Maid

Crisp mornings around the castle. I saw a lineup of birds, clothespinned to the telephone line outside my bedroom window. A rest stop on the way to Acapulco.

The children dress for school on the hearth, warmed by early flames and early cartoons.

I said: "Hurry up with your shoes! Everybody's about ready to go."

They said: "We're hurrying."

They *are* hurrying. But it is very hard to put on socks and shoes when you cannot see what you are doing. And how can you possibly see what you are doing when you are watching Bullwinkle?

I don't know why television stations put cartoons on right when people are supposed to be getting ready for school. Are they against education?

Why don't they put on farm shows, real estate shows, or the news during that hour? *That* would be public service broadcasting.

Lively times around the castle. I heard footsteps downstairs about 5:30 a.m. the other day. Padding around all over the place.

Went down and there was the 5-year-old cleaning the house. Picking up the living room. Emptying the dishwasher. Sweeping with a broom that was two-feet taller than her head.

She said: "I just woke up."

No explanation as to why she suddenly felt compelled to get into a flurry of housework. (I was too sleepy to question her.)

Her mother came down and told her to put on some shoes. She said: "If you couldn't sleep, why didn't you watch TV?"

She said: "There's nothing on but light."

I said: "What are we all doing, standing down here in the living room at 5:30 in the morning?"

One of those good questions that never quite get answered.

The household grinds into gear like a used car on these chilly mornings. Grr-rrr.

"I can't find my sweater."

"Did somebody take my brush?"

"Who's in the bathroom *now*?"

"Didn't you get any coffee when you shopped yesterday?" (That one starts the panic light glowing bright red.)

A lot of everybody's life around here seems to be spent in hurrying to get someplace they don't want to go in the first place. School, work, the store, the dentist, etc., etc., etc.

My wife said: "I think man really is cut out for the four-day week. By the end of five days, I'm pooped. Then we have to spend two days getting ready for the *next* five days."

I said: "I am more in favor of the four-day weekend." (I am even *more* in favor of the seven-day weekend.)

"Idle hands are the devil's workshop," Grandma used to say. (Grandma was full of that kind of stuff.)

Fifth Grade Politics

The general election is barely over, and we are already back in the thick of political intrigues. The fifth grader is running for school vice-president.

"I have to write a campaign speech," he said. I said: "Well, now . . ."

His mother interrupted. "We can look it over for you, but it will have to be your own words. That's only fair."

(Some politician she'd make.)

She said: "How long does it have to be?"

He said: "Well, there's five others running for vice-president, so we only get a minute each."

It sounds like they are running this school election something like one of those "25 words or less" contests.

I said: "If it's not cheating, I'd like to suggest that you use part of your time to tell them your name—just so they'll know who to vote for in case they like you."

He said: "I've already got a start. How does this sound: "Friends, Romans and countrymen, lend me your ears . . ."

I said: "Are those really your own words? They sound vaguely familiar."

I do not recall having class elections in the fifth grade. I went to a rigid little Catholic grade school in Oregon, and democracy wasn't what we were there for.

I said: "What are your duties as vice-president?"

He said: "I don't know. I think we have to take messages to the office a lot. Stuff like that. Can you help me make some signs?"

I said: "Sure, I guess so. As long as you use your own words. Do you have any slogans yet?"

He said: "I've got one. How does this sound?" He handed me a piece of lined paper with his slogan printed on it.

"Don't Be A Rat! Vote For Matt!"

Well, we sat down in the smoke-filled room (the biscuits had burned again) and mapped out our eleventh hour strategy.

I said: "I'm afraid I couldn't write a good one minute campaign speech for you, even if it was fair. What you need is somebody from Reader's Digest."

An older brother said: "Why don't you run on a no homework platform."

Well, after about an hour on his stomach before the fireplace, the candidate finally came up with his speech.

First, as planned before, he asked for the loan of their ears. Then he gave his name in full. Then he said:

". . . and I have 10 brothers and sisters, so I think I am well qualified to get along with a lot of kids. So, don't be a rat, vote for Matt!"

It's a story of democracy in action.

Days of Wine-red Noses

Cooler days now. A little change in temperatures and half the troops come down with colds and mild flu. When I left for work, the living room looked like a field hospital.

Some people stayed in their own rooms, but the living room was the general ward.

(People who stay in their own rooms are *really* sick. The living room is where the color television is.)

I said: "See, that's what you get for wearing sandals to school in November."

This does not get through to them. They cannot make the connection between cold feet and a head cold.

I said: "Dum dum. The cold weather travels up your legs then up your spine like a bad news telegram. When it hits your head—Bonk!"

We tried the vitamin C route. I had them taking them like they were cocktail peanuts.

Still, they woke up this morning with heads so clogged you'd think they had been downing the cocktails.

I said: "All right. Stay home from school. But rest and don't get into any riots."

(Going home after the children have been alone there all day is a little like opening a surprise package.)

Science and I have been trying to cure the common cold for years. Science has a bigger research budget, but I still figure we are about even.

Science pushes tiny little time capsules that explode in your system like ladyfinger firecrackers every hour or so.

I push a slug of .100 caliber whiskey in a glass of hot lemonade. A single, sudden explosion. Then a good night's sleep.

Science's patients may have drier noses. But mine have bigger smiles on their faces when they hit the sack.

"Feed a cold, starve a fever." That was Grandma's motto. (She had a lot of mottos, that dear old lady.)

One of her cold cures was the mustard plaster. She took

some kind of concoction that was hot enough to burn through a safe, and wrapped it like a bandage around your chest.

I think the idea was to *melt* the cold germs.

On the other children in the family that did not have colds, she hung an asafetida bag around their necks.

This was not to cure colds. This was preventative medicine.

That bag of herbs was so foul smelling, even people with head colds could smell it and retch. Nobody with germs—in fact, nobody at all—would come near the person wearing one of those bags.

Grandma was ahead of both science and me.

Weekend in Albuquerque

The last time I saw Los Angeles, the sun was shining and the people were in their usual storm of life. Less than two hours later I was standing in the middle of a near blizzard in New Mexico among peaceful people.

"Flying ain't the way to get here, though," said Max Evans, the cowboy turned film maker, over the hottest bowl of chili that has ever immolated my insides.

"I always take the train," he said.

"It's a good long ride, and you need that much time to iron out the kinks that Los Angeles can put in your stomach.

"Besides, I'm a jinx to mechanical things. Something goes wrong with every blame mechanical thing I put my foot in. I sure don't want to start messing up engines at 18,000 feet."

He yelled out to the kitchen: "Pat, honey, is there any more chili. Bring ol' John and me some more chili."

This was the next morning at the home of Pat and Max Evans. We were at breakfast.

He said: "Is there anything wrong, old buddy? Your eyes look like they're watering."

I said: "No Max, nothing. Pat, could I have another tall glass of water?"

These New Mexico people are certainly warm inside. And

they spread the feeling around when you sit down at their tables.

Bits of snow outside, and a warm fireplace in a room full of Navajo rugs on the inside. Max and I had just met a month before to begin work on a little mutual project. Now we were trying to get to know each other better. Each man trying to get inside the other's skull.

We sat up talking until after 4 a.m. We mentally made a half-dozen great movies, four or five best sellers, assorted short stories, and maybe a poem or two thrown in. And, sure enough, over the chili the next morning, our skulls felt considerably different.

After breakfast, we looked outside.

No snow had stuck to the streets of the city, but the Sandia Mountains outside of town were painted white.

"Well, let's have some more coffee," said Max. "Then I want to take you up to see my mine. We don't mine it, anymore, but it's a lot of fun to poke around up there."

He said it was up near "that government place where they got all those hydrogen bombs buried in the mountain," and added that he thought maybe he would go shoot off a few sticks of dynamite up near his mine someday "just to watch the reaction."

A half hour later we crawled into his pickup truck. Max turned the key. Nothing. The generator was shot.

"See what I mean about mechanical things?" said Max.

We climbed in a sedan and, the minute the engine turned over, we heard a whistling noise. "Now, what the hell's that?" asked Max. "It's never done that before."

But the car ran, even with the whistle, and we drove through the streets of Albuquerque. "I hate to drive, anyway," said Max. "I'm so sorry at it."

I said: "For a man who has to travel so much, you sure have limited choices on how to do it."

I think Max could commute between New Mexico, Hollywood, New York and location points a lot better on horseback. Slower, but much more comfortable.

We pulled up to a small film studio a few minutes later. He said: "Since I couldn't take you up to see the mountains, I'm going to show you a little film about them."

It was a beautiful 30-minute documentary called "Everyman's Mountain," which showed the Sandias in all four seasons of the year, and stressed a plea not to ruin them with houses, transmitting towers, beer cans and chain saws.

It was a poem of a film. And the projector only broke down three times.

Lights in the Pepper Tree

Chilly winds whipping around our December corners. We've battened all the hatches except one. The cat door in the kitchen swings back and forth like the Last Chance Saloon.

You could hang meat in our kitchen, until someone gets up and turns on the oven.

It's getting very Christmasy around here. I strung a lot of blinking lights in the pepper tree in back. It gives a nice effect of colored fireflies.

We bought a Santa Claus that lights up for the piano top. A poinsettia for a center piece. The Christmas cards are lined up on a shelf along the wall.

All this preparation is causing a lot of stress on the nervous systems of younger members of the family.

They are going to die if they have to wait much longer. I mean, absolutely *die.*

"Couldn't we open just one present?" they said.

I said: "For goodness' sake, what kind of spirit is that? Christmas is still two weeks away."

(I get a little antsy, too. But I figure we'll have to wait a couple more days, anyway.)

We haven't made a country run for our mistletoe, yet. But I know where to find some. I staked it out earlier this fall.

The custom of kissing under the mistletoe originated with the ancient Druids. In those days it had to be cut with a golden knife.

Last year our daughters put mistletoe *everywhere* in the house.

They had little sprigs hanging from a dozen places in the living room, the hallway, the den.

There was mistletoe hanging over the kitchen sink.

There was mistletoe hanging in some places I won't even tell you about.

Then, when their brothers brought friends over the girls would go about the house screeching to each other: "*Eeeekkkk!* Watch out! You're under the mistletoe."

None of the boys ever took the hint. Alas.

The children are coming home from college. One by plane, one by train. (They go to the same university, but they go their separate ways.)

My wife had a dream about talking to the son on his plans.

She said: "You know, I dreamed he called and I asked him how he was going to get home. Then he told me to wait a while so he could check rides to the airport with some friends.

"Then he just *left* me there, hanging onto the phone, running up the phone bill. He must have been away from the phone for 15 minutes. Isn't that just like him?"

I said: 'For goodness' sake, you are bumrapping the kid for something he did in *your* dream. Isn't that kind of weird?"

She said: "I suppose so, but it *is* just like him."

On the Edge—and Edgy

We are sitting on the edge of Christmas, and people couldn't be much edgier. "How many more days *now*?" wailed the youngest.

It's a question asked and answered daily.

She said: "A boy at nursery school said today was Christmas, but it isn't. *Is* it?" (Maybe an outside chance?)

I said: "Only eight more days to go."

She said: "Eight isn't very many. *Is* it?"

Somebody once said: "Anticipation is half the fun." (Maybe it was Grandma. It sounds like her.)

However, that depends on who's doing the anticipating and what's being anticipated.

When a 5-year-old cupcake is waiting for Christmas, the anticipation can drive her up the wall. (Not to mention the people around her.)

She said: "You know what time I'm going to bed the day before Christmas. Three o'clock."

She is not talking about staying up to catch Santa, friends. She is talking about three o'clock in the *afternoon*!

We drove off into the chilly evening to see the lights of Christmas. The sound of carols poured out into the night air. Peace on Earth. (But *where* on Earth?)

Through the lights of Balboa Park, strung across the Laurel Street Bridge. A stroll through the Nativity scenes in the Organ Pavilion.

We drove around behind the Ford Building to catch a splendid view of the downtown decorations. Then back through the park to the spot where Santa's sleigh is taking off with Rudolph in the lead.

This youngest moppet now knows *all* the words to "Rudolph the Red-nosed Reindeer." And she hasn't stopped singing it since Thanksgiving. (Except to ask how many more days *now*?)

Do not interrupt her. Do not sing along with her. If you do, she stops and starts it all over again at the beginning.

She knows all the words. But only from top to bottom.

Santa Claus is coming to nursery school next Monday. "It's not really Christmas," she said. "But he's too busy to come on Christmas day."

I said: "That's understandable. Besides, the place is closed, isn't it?"

She said: "Yeah. You know what Jerry said? He said Santa Claus is really only your mother and father? Jerry is in the first grade."

I said: "Who are you going to believe, some smarty first-grader or a veteran newspaper reporter who has been through two wars and lived in Boston?"

She said: "I told Jerry he didn't know *any*thing. There is *too* a Santa Claus. *Isn't* there?"

I said: "You hit it right on the nose, kiddo."

It was a song cue.

"Ru-dolph the red-nosed rein-deer, hadda very shiney no-o-se . . ."

Sunshine and birdsong. I talked to a friend in Manhattan on the phone and he said New York City was warm, sunny and clear as San Diego.

(Of course, he also said he had just returned from a three-martini luncheon.)

We are packing for the snow country around here. Next week some of us will spend a few days vacation in peaceful Idyllwild.

"Shall I pack your typewriter?" she asked.

I said: "Are you kidding? Just give it a swift kick and put it in a dark corner."

What kind of idea is that? I intend to lash myself to a big armchair in front of a roaring fire and watch the snow drifts pile up outside.

Just having that blasted machine along would make me feel uneasy.

We still have Christmas and three birthdays to get through before we can head for the hills. Some pressure has been put on me to get a dog for Christmas.

I said: "What do we need a dog for? We've got three cats."

They said: "Aw, the cats are for the girls. We've got a fenced-yard again. Why can't we have a dog? You could write about him."

That's true. I could write humorous little essays on how he tipped over the garbage cans. Clever little pieces on how he dug up the flower beds.

I could probably have people in the aisles by reporting how he chewed up my shoes.

I said: "How about if we got another desert tortoise? They don't do anything, and sleep half the year."

We once had a desert tortoise—Barstow Bill. He was a wonderful animal, and displayed almost no signs of life except one spring when he fell in love with a toy army helmet.

The rest of the time, Bill was just there. Oh, he moved. We knew that, because we would find him in different places from time to time in the back yard.

But we rarely *saw* him move.

And in the winter months, he would pull inside himself and hibernate. (We could have made a lamp out of him, and he would never have known the difference.)

Bill was strong as a small tank. One day he disappeared, and we found a hole in the board fence.

Bill had simply crashed through to freedom.

We don't know why he left. Perhaps to look for another helmet.

After all, it was spring. And Bill couldn't have been more than 50 years old.

Apologies to Clement Moore

'Twas the night before Christmas, and all through the castle, the moppets, as usual, continued to hassle.

The stockings were hung by the fireside in rows.

(I said: "No, it's not fair to hang up panty-hose!")

The children were sitting up, watching TV; the cats were both trying to knock down the tree.

While Mom in her bathrobe, from the back bathroom swishes, demanding: "Okay, now, whose turn to do dishes?"

"It's Mark's," says Katie. "It is not," he replies. "It's Julie's." (Julie turns. She has fire in her eyes.)

"I did them *last* night! I won't do them again!"

I look at my wife. I say: "Where is the gin?"

When all of a sudden, from out on the lawn, I hear this loud clatter. (Rover stifles a yawn.)

I rush to the window; I'm there in a flash.

I whip open the drapes. (And darn near break the sash.)

There on the sidewalk, a small figure appears, with a grin wide enough it connects up his ears.

With a little round tummy, and whiskers of white; a strange apparition on this Christmas Eve night.

There midst the trash of a whole week he stands. He's a neighborhood dog. He's knocked over the cans.

"Now dash it! Now dammit! Now hurry!" I stress; "Now Matthew! Now Stacey! Let's clean up this mess.

"On Marko! On Michael! Come Julie! Come Sean! That dog has strewn garbage all over the lawn!"

But the pooch, he just stood there, his nose in the sky; a bone in his teeth and a spark in his eye.

Dressed all in fur, from his head to his toe. (What else? That's the way all dogs dress up, you know.)

He wiggled his tail, that long-eared canine sinner, as if to say "Thanks, for the Christmas Eve dinner."

With the drop of the bone, to the first child he ran, and then started licking the back of his hand.

I started to reach for a stick on a shelf, then I just began laughing, in spite of myself.

I continued to chuckle, as I picked up the lids. This pure-blooded mongrel had captured the kids.

They were on the ground petting, and stroking his ear. "He looks like he's homeless. Can we keep him here?"

I said: "No. He belongs to some kids round the bend. But, since he's a neighbor, we should ask him in."

So, into the house, like a bullet he flies. Galloping! Panting! "Hi cats, and hi guys!"

He knocks over a table, and breaks it, I think. About as much grace as an old Sherman tank.

He's full of high spirits and holiday glee.

I yelled: "Keep that mongrel away from the tree!"

The cats disappear underneath a near bed, and the pooch just keeps running. Not a brain in his head.

But we settle him down, with a piece of cold liver.

He quits running in circles, but continues to quiver.

"Let's give him some cookies, and ice cream," they say. (We don't get a weird dog in his house every day.)

When he finally gets filled, he looks somewhat sore; and his tummy is twice as round as before.

So we hug him, and pet him, and open the door. And he shoots out as fast as he shot in before.

And he barks and he wiggles as he runs out of sight, as if to be saying "Happy Christmas tonight!"

(But I do think I saw him eye the trash with a grin, as if to say, "Maybe I'll try this again.")

A Christmas Night Story

Long ago, in the days before history books, and far away, in a green, hidden valley, there lived a curious little people known as The Widgets.

Now, Widgets all came in about the same size—somewhere under three feet tall. But they were different in other ways. Some were a lovely pale color. Some were a beautiful dark color, dark as the deepest shade in their valley. Some seemed to be tinted an almost-red, while others were nearly as yellow as turning aspen leaves.

Of course, there were other Widgets, with in-between hues. Some had blond hair, some had black, and some had bright, fiery red. Some were almost bald.

A lot of them had freckles around their noses, especially the ones with bright, fiery red hair.

Widgets behaved in the strangest ways. Sometimes they would laugh, and you wouldn't know why. Sometimes, for no reason you could guess, they would just start crying.

They certainly walked funny enough—a little, bow-legged sort of gait. And they dearly loved to get messed up. Why, you could bathe and dress Widget fresh as Sunday, and in minutes they would have peanut butter or something on their faces and clothes, and probably in their hair.

The Widgets' diet consisted mostly of fresh milk and cookies and creamed Widget foods that came in small tins. However, they were known to dine on mud pies and crayons from time to time, and were perfectly willing to try eating almost anything they could reach.

Now, if there was anything in the world the Widgets loved better than laughing and cookies and mudpies, it was to be picked up and held tightly.

And this was the only sad thing about the green, hidden valley. For nowhere in it was there anybody big enough or strong enough to pick up a Widget and hold it tightly.

And it so happened, there was another valley two or three hills away in which lived another kind of strange and curious people called The Big People.

The Big People came in all shapes, sizes and colors, too, but were very different from the Widgets in other ways.

The Big People did not laugh as much, but neither did they cry as much. They preferred being what they called Serious.

They tried to play Big People games, but they never managed to have nearly as much fun as The Widgets. They wouldn't think of walking around with peanut butter on their faces. They rarely drank milk. And the idea of eating a mud pie made them sick.

They spent most of their time working and worrying and trying to be bigger than the other Big People and making payments.

Watching over both of these valleys, the valley of The Widgets and the valley of The Big People, was someone called Someone who lived in a place called Someplace. And he was concerned.

He called a few of the people who worked for him and they had a conference.

"Why is it," said Someone, "that the Widgets feel they need to be picked up and held tightly?"

"Well, sir," said one of Someone's vice presidents, "the only thing we can figure is that since the dictionary says 'Widget' means 'small attachment,' we have a bunch of small attachments on our hands with nothing for them to attach to."

A committee of vice presidents then stepped forward and said: "We suggest The Widgets be passed out to The Big

People in the other valley, who are strong enough to pick them up and hold them tightly."

Someone said: "What? Do you think The Big People can be trusted with Widgets? What with all their worrying?"

The committee said: "Well, at least The Widgets would be something for The Big People to worry *about*. As it is, they go around most of the time worrying about nothing."

"That's true," said Someone. "Also, maybe they could help keep The Widgets a little cleaner, and try to keep them from eating anything more dangerous than mud pies. Still, The Widgets are a big responsibility. I don't know if The Big People are really qualified to handle them."

The committee said: "That may be true, sir. But the problem is, there simply isn't anyone else."

So the plan was tried. The Widgets were passed out by ones, twos, threes and more to The Big People. They came with instruction booklets on how to feed them creamed Widget food, how to bathe them, and how to pick them up and hold them tightly.

And how did the plan work? Well, it didn't come out perfect, but it wasn't too bad. The Widgets didn't make The Big People stop worrying. And they even added a few payments to be made each month.

But The Widgets did make The Big People laugh a little more often, and cry a little more often. And The Big People finally had something to really worry about.

In return, The Big People once in awhile would pick up one of his Widgets and hold it tightly. And when they did that, it didn't matter what else was wrong with The Big People, The Widgets loved them.

And the best night of all each year was Christmas night, after The Widgets had the peanut-butter scrubbed off their faces and were sound asleep.

The Big People then would sit back in their chairs, by the fireplace, and one of them would say to the other: "Isn't all this good? I wonder who planned this whole thing, anyway?"

And the other would say: "Someone, I guess."